Object-Oriented Client/Server
Application Development

Systems Design and Implementation Series

To order or receive additional information on these or any other McGraw-Hill titles, in the United States please call 1-800-822-8158. In other countries, contact your local McGraw-Hill representative. **BC14BCZ**

Object-Oriented Client/Server Application Development

Using ObjectPAL and C++

Steve J. Ayer

McGraw-Hill, Inc.

New York   San Francisco   Washington, D.C.   Auckland   Bogotá
Caracas   Lisbon   London   Madrid   Mexico City   Milan
Montreal   New Delhi   San Juan   Singapore
Sydney   Tokyo   Toronto

Library of Congress Cataloging-in-Publication Data

Ayer, Steve J., (date)
 Object-oriented client/server application development using
ObjectPAL and C++ / Steve J. Ayer
     p.   cm.
   Includes index
   ISBN 0-07-002861-3
   1. Client/server computing. 2. Object-oriented programming
 (Computer science) 3. ObjectPAL (Computer program language)
 4. C++ (Computer program language) I. Title.
 QA76.9C65A94 1995
 005.75′8—dc20   94-24430
                                                                 CIP

  2 3 4 5 6 7 8 9 0   DOC/DOC   9 0 9 8 7 6 5

ISBN 0-07-002861-3

*The sponsoring editor for this book was Jerry Papke, the editing
supervisor was Caroline R. Levine, and the production supervisor was
Suzanne Rapcavage. This book was set in Century Schoolbook by
McGraw-Hill's Professional Book Group composition unit.*

Printed and bound by R. R. Donnelley & Sons Company.

Contents

Preface

Both object-oriented and client/server architectures are increasing in popularity as more and more organizations install networks to share resources in a distributed database environment. The purpose of this book is to view these concepts from the perspective of two different programming language environments: (1) an object-oriented programming language environment in which programmers can create their own object types, and (2) an object-based programming language environment in which only those object types defined by the programming language can be used. The author has selected C++ (an object-oriented programming language) and ObjectPAL (an object-based programming language) to demonstrate the differing impacts of these two programming languages in an object-oriented client/server computing environment.

Object-Oriented Client/Server Application Development Using ObjectPal and C++ provides practical guidelines and procedures for planning, managing, developing, and controlling the developed product and its documentation. These guidelines and procedures define a system life cycle within which all the required development work can take place. The first part of the book analyzes the architectures for object-oriented and client/server computing and presents a methodological framework for systems development. The second part of the book presents a methodology for systems analysis, design, implementation, and testing. The third part of the book identifies products that provide technical support in developing and implementing an object-oriented client/server system.

This book presents an *object-oriented methodology*. That is to say, it defines an approach to developing computer applications from an object-oriented perspective. The applications developed using this approach may or may not be object based. That will depend both on the design and on the language in which the design is implemented. Object-oriented analysis and design do, through use cases and encapsulation of data and functionality, force us into viewing application components in terms of the environment in which they will operate—whether or not they are implemented using an object-oriented language.

The book should be of particular interest to executives whose activities interrelate with the systems development function; to practitioners who bear the direct responsibility for planning, developing, and implementation of computer systems; and to serious students of information systems processing.

Steve J. Ayer

Acknowledgments

I wish to extend thanks to my many friends and colleagues for their contributions to the preparation of this manuscript. These include the people at On-Command Video in Santa Clara, California, especially Brian Barnett and Carol Bowen; and the people in the information systems department at Coors Brewery in Golden, Colorado, with whom I have shared many hours discussing systems development methodologies.

I especially wish to recognize the talents and efforts of Frank Patrinostro, a colleague with whom I have co-authored other works. Without his professional advice and assistance in researching the subject matter of this book the task of preparing the manuscript would have been far more difficult. In addition I would also like to extend my special thanks to Jerry Papke, senior editor at McGraw-Hill for making the publication of this book possible.

I would also like to acknowledge Borland International for providing me with information resources regarding ObjectPAL and C++, upon which portions of the methodology presented herein were based.

List of Abbreviations

4GL	Fourth Generation Language
AFP	AppleTalk Filing Protocol
ANSI	American National Standards Institute
API	application program interface
BLOB	binary large object
BOCA	Borland Object Component Architecture
CASE	computer-aided software engineering
CD-ROM	compact disk read-only memory
CUA	Common User Access
CVMU	Carnegie-Mellon University Package
DBMS	database management system
DDBMS	Distributed Database Management System
DDL	data definition language
DDP	datagram delivery protocol
DLL	dynamic link library
DTM	Distributed Transaction Manager
GUI	graphical user interface
I/O	input/output
ICMP	Internet Control Message Protocol
ICS	InstantCom Communications Server
IDAPI	Integrated Database Application Programming Interface
IDE	integrated development environment
IDP	Internetwork Datagraph Protocol
IP	Internet Protocol
IPX	Internetwork Packet Exchange
IS	information systems
LAN	local area network

MIB	management information base
MIS	management information systems
NACS	NetWare Asynchronous Communication Server
NCP	NetWare Core Protocol
NFS	network file system
ODI	open datalink interface
OLTP	online transaction processing
OOA	object-oriented analysis
OOD	object-oriented design
OODBMS	object-oriented database management system
OOP	object-oriented programming
OOUI	object-oriented user interface
OS	operating system
OSI	open systems interconnection
PC	personal computer
PEP	packet exchange protocol
QBE	query by example
RDBMS	relational database management system
RIP	routing information protocol
RPC	remote procedure call
SAA	Systems Application Architecture
SAP	service advertising protocol
SNMP	Simple Network Management Protocol
SPP	sequenced packet protocol
SPX	sequenced packet exchange
SQL	structured query language
STP	shielded twisted pair
TACS	Telebit Asynchronous Communications Server
TCP	Transmission Control Protocol
TCP/IP	Transmission Control Protocol/Internet Protocol
UART	universal asyncronous receiver/transmitter
UDP	User Datagram Protocol
UI	user interface
UTP	unshielded twisted pair
XNS	Xerox Network Systems

Overview of Object-Oriented Client/Server Computing

Part 1 of this book provides an overview of the basics of object-oriented client/server computing. It serves as the framework on which the rest of the book is based.

Chapter 1, Object-Oriented Computing Concepts, *provides an overview of the basic concepts of object-oriented computing. It summarizes how objects are encapsulated into classes and instances, describes how properties of one class may be inherited from another class, and explains how polymorphism enables an instance to communicate with another instance without knowing its class. It also analyzes how these basic concepts can be applied to applications development in two programming language environments: C++ and ObjectPAL.*

In Chapter 2, The Client/Server Computing Environment, *each element of the client/server computing environment is reviewed: resource sharing, distributed processing, relational database, network connectivity, and network management issues. In addition, the role of Structured Query Language (SQL) as an essential link in client/server computing is summarized and an overview of the Open System Interconnection (OSI) standards for network development is provided.*

Chapter 3, Object-Oriented Client/Server Development Framework, *presents a methodological outline for object-oriented client/server applications development using ObjectPAL and C++. It serves as the foundation for the methodology detailed in Part 2.*

1

Object-Oriented
Computing Concepts

Object-oriented analysis (OOA), *object-oriented design* (OOD), and *object-oriented programming* (OOP) are evolutionary steps in the science of computer applications development. They differ from traditional development techniques in several areas, but the roots of the technology are very evident in the traditional methods and standards of well-structured development organizations. The revolutions in computer technology have permitted the evolution of application development methods. Early computer technologies were limited by memory and input/output (I/O) constraints to handle only batch jobs and were used primarily in automating accounting functions. The original applications were developed in assembly language and required considerable machine-specific knowledge to write.

As computing capacities increased and file storage and access methods improved, high-order languages such as FORTRAN, COBOL, and RPG were developed. These technology improvements enabled the developers to begin to create and use standard library utilities for data routines, sort procedures, and other common functions.

Improvements in communications and timesharing technologies allowed for development of on-line systems where users could access applications from their desks. This dramatically increased the number of persons using the systems and meant that data-processing organizations had to begin thinking in terms of user interfaces rather than only job flows. The increased number of users also resulted in an increase in the number of change requests and enhancements, which began to strain the capacities of the development staff.

The introduction of minicomputers, followed by personal computers, brought computing technology to virtually every desktop. The rate of change in the technology and the ready availability of applications to run on personal computers (PCs) created enormous expectations on the part of the end users. Parallel to the changes in technology, the rate of change in the business community imposes changes on applications requirements. This environment of rapid change is forcing changes in the way computer applications are developed.

Traditional systems development methodologies have one common feature—development is a linear process which begins with an analysis phase that culminates with the publication of a requirements specification document. This document establishes the baseline for the application design, programming, and testing. Unfortunately, the time between publications of the requirements specification and the delivery of the completed application could take months or years! With the rate of change in the business environment, this often means that systems are outdated before they are implemented. The complexity of the programming structures often makes the prospect of revising the systems to meet the new requirements as big a task as the original development.

An object-oriented development methodology resolves this problem because

- Object-oriented development is *iterative*—therefore, adaptable to changing requirements.

- Objects are *self-contained*—therefore, changes are easier to isolate and faster to implement.

- Objects model *real-world entities*—allowing requirements to be more easily understood.

The remainder of this chapter explains the terms and basic concepts of object-oriented development. This book describes a methodology for developing object-oriented systems. It should be emphasized, however, that object-oriented development is an evolutionary step in applications development and is itself still evolving. The specifics of the programming language you select and the tools you have available will drive your implementation of object-oriented technology. Also remember that using an object-oriented language does not guarantee the development of object-oriented systems. Such systems result from object-oriented designs.

There is no universally accepted definition of what constitutes an object-oriented programming language. However, it is generally agreed that object-oriented languages provide support for object encapsulation, instantiation, inheritance, and polymorphism. This chapter briefly explains all these concepts and describes their implementation in two programming language environments: C++ and ObjectPAL.

The Object Environment

In a traditional structured methodology, analysts, design engineers, and programmers focus on the data flow between the computer processes. In an object computing environment, the developers and users alike must deal with objects that represent real-world entities and the messages or events that elicit actions from these objects. The languages and compilers or interpreters used for creating and manipulating objects and for communications among the objects provide the tools that are needed to generate compiled applications. The elements that distinguish object-oriented computing from traditional procedural computing are object identification and abstraction, encapsulation, polymorphism, and inheritance.

Object identification and abstraction

In object computing, an *object* is an abstraction of a real-world entity defined by its procedures or informational characteristics. The object may be an abstraction of a tangible thing, a role or assignment to be performed, an incident that occurs, an interaction between two or more entities, or a set of rules and standards that must be followed. For example, in an export processing application, a *tangible object* may be abstraction of the physical product to be exported, an *assignment object* may be an abstraction of the freight forwarder who is responsible for packing and shipping the product, an *incident object* may be an abstraction of the functions that must be performed by the importer at the port of entry, an *interaction object* may be an abstraction of the commercial invoice that accompanies the shipment, and a *rules object* may be an abstraction of the export regulation which must be adhered to by the exporter.

When thinking of objects, one must expand the concept of entities used in data modeling to include not only data and data attributes but also procedures. An object can be thought of as an entity that encapsulates both the data and the program code that generates the actions of the object. These object operations are sometimes called *methods*.

Objects are identified by first analyzing the operations to be performed by the application that is under development. Each object

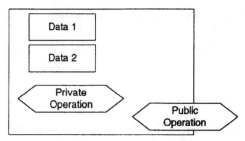

Figure 1.1 Example of behavioral and informational data that characterize an object.

identified is then characterized by its attributes. The next step is to formalize the relationships among objects. These relationships are defined in terms of the states of instances of one object in relation to the states of other object instances. Thus, all the information that affects object-oriented computing is contained within the objects. The abstracted objects become the entities that provide for the operations in the object-oriented computing environment.

Since the behavior of each abstracted object is encapsulated in the object, all that is seen of the object is its interface with the rest of the application. Thus, the behavior of the object is hidden from view and can be manipulated only when an object is called on to perform a specific operation. Figure 1.1 illustrates certain data that characterize an object.

Classes and instances

A review of the literature will show an inconsistency in the use of the term *object*. Some authors refer to an object as a single instance of a real-world entity. For example, the object may be a particular student. Other authors use the term *object* as a generalized reference and create single *instances* to represent a particular student. In the second approach the terms *object* and *class* may be used interchangeably. This book will not attempt to resolve the inconsistency. However, the word *object* in this book will most frequently be used in the first sense. Thus the object will be equated to an instance.

Every object that is a member of a certain class is referred to as an *instance*. Each instance has a unique identifier. The current state of the instance is defined by the operations performed on the instance (see Fig. 1.2).

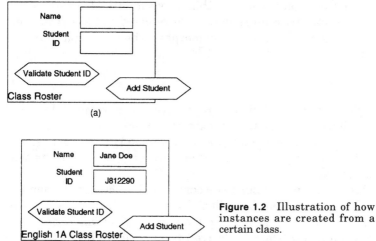

(a)

(b)

Figure 1.2 Illustration of how instances are created from a certain class.

Polymorphism

The term *polymorphism* is a biology term used to describe how related organisms can assume a variety of forms. In object-oriented development, instances are created from classes. Instances from different classes may share similar functions. Thus, another object can communicate to an instance of unknown class using a single message (not class-specific). This ability to send stimuli to instances of unknown class is called *polymorphism*. In an object-oriented language environment, a single operation may be implemented using polymorphic methods. Certain objects addressed by pointers (see example in Fig. 1.3) thus can change form, depending on the run-

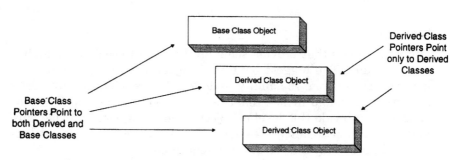

Figure 1.3 Base class pointers can address derived-class objects.

time class of the object. Classes that have identical interfaces to serve different specific requirements are referred to as *polymorphic classes*. In C++ a class becomes polymorphic when a virtual function is declared.

Inheritance

When we identify different classes that have many common data and operational characteristics, we can extract the common components to create separate classes—one having the common characteristics, and one for each of the original classes that have only those aspects that make them unique.

These classes can now inherit the common characteristics from the new class. New classes can be built from existing classes using a feature of object-oriented programming languages called *inheritance* (see Fig. 1.4). When a new class is derived from a single base class, the process is called *single inheritance*. When a new class inherits the data members and member functions from more than one base class, it is called *multiple inheritance*.

Development Concepts

The information system (IS) organizations which are choosing the object-oriented paradigm are motivated by several factors, most importantly quality, development and maintenance productivity, system flexibility, and reuse. When analyzed, the primary driver of the quality and productivity is the ability to reuse objects. Encapsulation of procedure and data does enhance the ability to control changes and especially control the impact of changes. Achievement of these benefits, however, requires the organizations to shift the way application development is managed. This includes new tools, languages, and methodologies.

Languages

Many languages that provide some level of object-oriented capability are available. The biggest benefit of object-oriented development, however, comes from the ability to define classes to encapsulate data and procedures and invoke inheritance and polymorphism. Few languages can provide this level of object orientation; most provide only part of this functionality. C++ and SmallTalk are the principal languages in use today that meet these requirements.

Development time has been shown to be reduced with the imple-

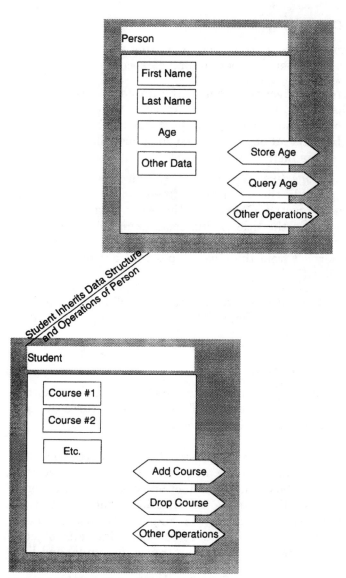

Figure 1.4   Process of inheritance.

mentation of visual programming tools. Toolkits and frameworks for the visual development of graphical user interfaces (GUIs) are prevalent, but the computer-aided software engineering (CASE) tools necessary to support visual programming are not commonly available.

Programming Concepts

The programming concepts of object computing are viewed in this subsection from two different programming perspectives:

Object-oriented perspective: When using an object-oriented programming language, programmers can create their own object types. *C++,* one of the programming languages referred to in the title of this book, is an object-oriented language that allows programmers to create their own object types.

Object-based perspective: When using an object-based programming language, only those objects defined by the programming language can be created. *ObjectPAL,* the other programming language referred to in the title of this book, is an object-based programming language. It limits the creation of objects to only those that can be derived from the object types that are predefined by the language itself.

We will review the features and characteristics of both C++ (object-oriented programming) and ObjectPAL (object-based programming) in the paragraphs that follow.

Object-oriented elements of C++

This subsection reviews concepts related to the C++ language structure: declarations, pointers, arrays, functions, structures, unions, enumerations, expressions, and statements.

Declarations. *Declarations* are the instructions in source code that identify a resource or value that the program will use during execution. Some declarations establish the creation of an object, the allocation of physical memory, and the possible initialization. Other declarations simply make information available to the compiler. The discussion that follows reviews the Borland C++ declarations relative to objects, storage classes and type, scope, duration, translation units, and linkage.

Borland C++ defines an *object* as an identifiable region of memory that can hold a fixed or variable value or set of values. (It should be noted that this definition differs from the more general use of the term in object-oriented languages.) Each value has an associated name that is used to access the object. The name may be a simple identifier or a complex expression that points to the object. Declarations establish the necessary mapping between identifiers and objects.

Each identifier must have at least two attributes: storage class and data type. The *storage class* enables the C++ compiler to deduce the location of the object and its life cycle. The *data type* determines how much memory is allocated to an object and how the program will interpret the bit patterns that are found in the object's storage allocations.

The *scope* of an identifier is that part of the program in which the identifier can be used to access its object. There are five categories of scope: block, function, function prototype, file, and class. The *block scope* starts at the declaration point and ends at the end of the block containing the declaration. The *function scope* consists of statement labels. Identifiers declared with the list of parameter declarations in a function prototype have a *function prototype scope*. *File scope identifiers* are declared outside all blocks and classes. Their scope is from the point of declaration to the end of the source file. *Class scope* applies to the names of the members of a particular class.

Duration, which is closely related to storage class, defines the period during which the declared identifiers have real, physical objects allocated in memory. There are three kinds of duration: static, local, and dynamic. *Static-duration objects* usually reside in fixed data segments allocated according to the memory model in force. All functions, wherever defined, are objects with static duration. *Local-duration objects* are created on the stack when the enclosing block or function is entered. They are deallocated when the program exits that block or function. *Dynamic-duration objects* are created and destroyed by specific function calls during a program. They are allocated from a special memory reserve.

A *translation unit* is the source code file together with any included files, but less any source lines omitted by conditional preprocessor directives. Syntactically, a translation unit is defined as a sequence of external declarations. The word *external* refers to declarations made outside any function.

Linkage is the process that allows each instance of an identifier to be associated correctly with one particular object or function. All identifiers have one of three linkage attributes that are closely related to their scope: external linkage, internal linkage, or no linkage. Each instance of a particular identifier with *external linkage* represents the same object or function throughout the entire set of files and libraries that make up the program. Each instance of a particular identifier with *internal linkage* represents the same object or function within one file only. Identifiers with *no linkage* represent unique entities.

All six interrelated attributes (storage, classes, types, scope, duration, and linkage) are determined by declarations. As the name implies, a defining declaration performs both the duties of declaring and defining an operation.

Pointers. Just as a mailing address represents a postal destination, a *pointer* in a C++ program represents the address of information stored in memory. Pointers to C++ objects can be established and manipulated in various memory models. Pointers fall into two categories: pointers to objects and pointers to functions. A *pointer to an object* holds the address of that object. A *pointer to a function* holds the address to which control is transferred when that function is called. A pointer must be declared as pointing to some particular type, even if that type is void. A pointer or the pointed-at object can be declared with the **const** modifier. Anything declared as a **const** cannot have its value changed. Pointer arithmetic is limited to addition, subtraction, and comparison. Pointer types can be converted to other pointer types using the typecasting mechanism.

Arrays. An *array* consists of a contiguous region of storage exactly large enough to hold all its elements. Multidimensional arrays are constructed by declaring arrays of array type as shown in the following example:

```
int arrayname [5] [7];
```

This declaration declares the three-dimensional array arrayname. The array created by this declaration is represented in the following chart.

[0] [0]	[0] [1]	[0] [2]	[0] [3]	[0] [4]	[0] [5]	[0] [6]
[1] [0]	[1] [1]	[1] [2]	[1] [3]	[1] [4]	[1] [5]	[1] [6]
[2] [0]	[2] [1]	[2] [2]	[2] [3]	[2] [4]	[2] [5]	[2] [6]
[3] [0]	[3] [1]	[3] [2]	[3] [3]	[3] [4]	[3] [5]	[3] [6]
[4] [0]	[4] [1]	[4] [2]	[4] [3]	[4] [4]	[4] [5]	[4] [6]

If an expression is given in an array declarator, it must evaluate to a positive constant integer which equals the number of elements in the array.

Functions. Languages such as Pascal distinguish between procedures and *functions*. In C++, functions play both roles. Each program must have a single external function named main that marks the entry point of the program. The functions are declared as prototypes in header files or with program files. Functions are external by default.

They are accessed from within any file in the program and can be restricted by using the static storage class specifier. Functions are defined in source files or made available by linking precompiled libraries. A given function can be declared several times in a program if the declarations are compatible. Excluding C++ function overloading, only one definition of any given function is allowed. Declarators specify the type of each function parameter. The compiler uses this information to check function calls for validity. Function prototypes aid in documenting code. When a function takes two parameters, the function prototype makes this clear. The definition of a function consists of optional storage class specifiers (**extern** or **static**), a return type, optional modifiers, the name of the function, a parameter declaration list, and a function body representing the code to be executed when the function is called. The function is called with actual arguments placed in the same sequence as those contained in the function prototype. The arguments are converted to the declared types of the formal parameters as if by initialization.

Structures. A *structure* is a collection of one or more values of the same or different types. A structure in C++ is treated as a class type, except that the default access to a structure is public, as is the default for the base class. A structure is declared using the keyword **struct**. For example

```
struct mystruct {…}; mystruct is the tag to the structure
   .
   .
   .
struct mystruct s, *ps, arrs[10]
```

When the structure tag is omitted, the structure is *untagged*. Untagged structures are used to declare the identifiers to be of the given structure type, but additional objects of this type elsewhere cannot be declared.

Memory is allocated to a structure member by member. Structure tag names share the same name space with union tags and enumeration tags. Such tags must be uniquely named with the same scope.

Unions. A *union* is similar to a structure, except that union members overlay one another, so that only one member at a time can have valid information. Like structures, unions may be initialized in the declaration. The size of a union is equal to the size of its largest member. A union is declared with the keyword **union**.

A union that does not have a tag and is not used to declare a named object is called an *anonymous union*. Anonymous unions can't have member functions and at a file level must be declared static.

The general syntax for unions is similar to that for structures. The differences are that unions can contain bit fields (but only one can be active) and C++ union types cannot use the class access.

Enumerations. An *enumeration* specifies mnemonic identifiers for a set of integer values. An enumeration is declared with the keyword **enum**. A variable of enumerated type can contain only one of the list of enumerated values in the declaration. For example

```
enum months {jan, feb, mar, apr, may, jun, jul, aug, sept, oct, nov,
dec} curmonth;
```

declares an enumeration variable curmonth of type months which can be assigned any one of the values listed in the declaration, but no other value. One or more enumerators can be set to specific values with explicit integral initializers. The initializer can be any expression yielding an integer value.

Expressions and operators. *Expressions* (see examples listed in Table 1.1) are sequences of operators, operands, and punctuators that programs perform. They are evaluated according to certain conversion, grouping, associativity, and precedence rules that depend on the operators used; the presence of parentheses; and the data types of the operands.

The operators in C++ (see list in Table 1.2) include arithmetical and logical operators, bit-level manipulation operators, structure and union component access operators, and pointer operations for referencing and dereferencing. Borland C++ extensions offer additional operators for accessing class members and their objects, together with a mechanism for overloading operators that lets you redefine the action of any standard operators when applied to the objects of a given class.

Borland C++ provides for general functions that allow the *overloading* of certain standard C operators. It also lets you redefine the actions of most operators, so that they perform specified functions when used with objects of a particular class. Operator functions can be called directly, although they are usually invoked indirectly by the use of the overload operator.

Statements. *Statements* specify the flow of program control during program execution. They are executed sequentially in the order of appearance in the source code (see Table 1.3).

TABLE 1.1   Borland C++ Expressions

Primary-expression
  literal
  this
  :: identifier
  :: operator-function-name
  :: qualified-name
  (expression)
  name

Literal:
  integer-constant
  character-constant
  floating-constant
  string-literal

name:
  identifier
  operator-function-name
  conversion-function-name
  ~class-name
  qualified-name

qualified-name:
  qualified-name::name

postfix-expression:
  primary-expression
  postfix-expression [expression]
  postfix-expression
    (<expression-list>)
  simple-type-name
    (<expression-list>)
  postfix-expression.name
  postfix-expression -> name
  postfix-expression ++
  postfix-expression —
  const_cast<type-id>(expression)
  dynamic_cast<type-id>(expression)
  reinterpret_cat<type-id>(expression)
  static_cast<type-id>(expression)
  typeid(expression)
  typeid(type-name)

expression-list:
  assignment-expression
  expression-list

unary-expression
  postfix-expression
  ++unary-expression
  —unary-expression
  unary-operator cast-expression
  sizeof unary-expression
  sizeof(typename)
  allocation-expression
  deallocation-expression

unary-operator: one of
  & * + - ~ !

allocation-expression
  <::>**new**<placement>new-type-name
    <initializer>
  <::>**new**<placement>(type-name)
    <initializer>)

placement:
  (expression-list)

new-type-name:
  type-specifiers<new-declarator>

new-declarator:
  ptr-operator<new-declarator>
  new-declarator[<expression>]

deallocation-expression:
  <::>**delete** cast-expression
  <::>**delete** cast-expression

cast-expression:
  unary-expression
  (type-name) cast-expression

pm-expression:
  cast-expression
  pm-expression.*cast-expression
  pm-expression->*cast-expression

multiplicative-expression:
  pm-expression
  multiplicative-expression*pm-
    expression
  multiplicative-expression/pm-
    expression
  multiplicative-expression%pm-
    expression

additive-expression:
  multiplicative-expression
  additive-expression +
    multiplicative-expression
  additive-expression-
    multiplicative-expression

shift-expression:
  additive-expression
  shift-expression<<additive-
    expression
  shift-expression>>additive-
    expression
relational-expression:
  shift-expression
  relational-expression<shift-
    expression
  relational-expression>shift-
    expression
  relational-expression< = shift-
    expression

TABLE 1.1   Borland C++ Expressions (*Continued*)

```
relational-expression> = shift-
  expression
equality-expression:
relational-expression
equality expression = = relational-
  expression
  equality expression ! = relational-
  expression


AND-expression:
  equality-expression
  AND-expression & equality-
    expression


exclusive-OR-expression:
  AND-expression
  exclusive-OR-expression^AND-
    expression


inclusive-OR-expression:
  exclusive-OR-expression
  inclusive-OR-expression|exclusive-
    OR-expression


logical-AND-expression:
  inclusive-OR-expression
  logical-AND-expression &&
    inclusive-OR-expression
```

```
logical-OR-expression:
  inclusive-OR-expression
  inclusive-OR-expression|exclusive-
    OR-expression


conditional-expression:
  logical-OR-expression
  logical-OR-expression||logical-
    AND-expression


assignment-expression:
  conditional-expression
  unary-expression assignment-
    operator assignment-expression


assignment-operator: one of
  = * = / = % = + = =
  << = >> = & = ^ = | =


expression:
  assignment-expression
  expression, assignment-expression


constant-expression
  conditional-expression
```

TABLE 1.2   Associativity and Precedence of Borland C++ Operators

Operators	Associativity
() [] -> :: .	Left to right
! ~ + - ++ — & * (typecast)	Right to left
sizeof new delete typeid	Right to left
.* ->*	Left to right
* / %	Left to right
+ -	Left to right
<< >>>	Left to right
< < = > > =	Left to right
= = ! =	Left to right
&	Left to right
^	Left to right
|	Left to right
&&	Left to right
||	Left to right
?: (conditional expression)	Right to left
= * = / = % = + = - = & = ^ = | = << = >> =	Right to left
,	Left to right

TABLE 1.3   Borland C++ Statements

```
statement:                          selection-statement
  labeled-statement                   if (expression) statement
  compound statement                  if (expression) statement else
  expression-statement                  statement
  selection-statement                 switch (expression) statement
  iteration-statement
  jump-statement                    iteration-statement:
  asm-statement                       while (expression) statement
  declaration                         do statement while (expression)
                                      for (for-init-statement
labeled-statement:                      <expression>;<expression>)
  identifier : statement                statement
  case constant-expression : statement
  default : statement               for-init-statement:
                                      expression-statement
compound statement                    declaration
  { <declaration-list> <statement-
    list> }                         jump-statement:
                                      goto identifier
declaration-list                      continue ;
  declaration                         break ;
  declaration-list declaration        return <expression>;

statement-list:
  statement
  statement-list statement

expression-statement:
  <expression>;

asm-statement
  asm tokens newline
  asm tokens;
  asm {tokens;<tokens;> =
    <tokens;>
    }
```

A *block statement* is a list of statements enclosed within matching brackets ({ }). Syntactically, a block can be considered to be a single statement, but it also plays a role in the scoping of identifiers.

A *labeled statement* serves as an identifier for the unconditional **goto** statement. Label identifiers have their own name space and function scope.

An expression followed by a semicolon forms an *expression statement*. Borland C++ executes an expression statement by evaluating the expression. Most expression statements are assignment statements or function calls.

Selection statements select from alternative courses of action by testing certain values.

The *switch statement* allows for the transfer of control to one of several case-labeled statements, depending on the value of the switch expression.

Iteration statements let you loop a set of statements. They offer a concise method for scanning strings and other null-terminated data structures.

A *jump statement,* when executed, transfers control unconditionally. There are four such statements: **break, continue, goto**, and **return**. A **break** statement can be used only inside an iteration. It terminates the iterator or switch statement. A **continue** statement can also be used only inside an iteration statement. It transfers control to the test condition for while and do loops. The **goto** statement transfers control to the statement labeled label. Return statements terminate the execution function.

Object-based elements of ObjectPAL

ObjectPAL is the application programming language integrated with the Borland Paradox for Windows relational database environment. ObjectPAL is designed for Paradox users to create database applications, define menus, organize and structure tables, define the functions required, and deliver the application. Once an application has been delivered, any ObjectPAL code is hidden from the user, so the customization of Paradox is transparent.

ObjectPAL has two aspects: the *integrated development environment* (IDE) and the language itself. The IDE includes the ObjectPAL Editor, ObjectPAL Debugger, a mechanism for creating and playing scripts, and facilities for delivering completed applications to users. The language includes the built-in ObjectPAL code that defines how the object responds to events and the run-time library (predefined methods and procedures that operate on objects and data).

Creating Paradox applications involves placing objects in forms and writing ObjectPAL *methods* to define how those objects behave. Like C++, ObjectPAL is a *compiled* language. The ObjectPAL compiler translates the written code into machine code that a computer can execute. It translates all the code in a form at one time, rather than interpreting each instruction just before it executes.

ObjectPAL creates compiled applications from the object types in Table 1.4.

Events.   *Events* are object types that set ObjectPAL in motion (see list in Table 1.5). An event consists of data and code that defines the kind of action that takes place (e.g., mouse click or keypress), precisely

TABLE 1.4   ObjectPAL Categories and Object Types

Category	Types
Events	ActionEvent, ErrorEvent, Event, KeyEvent, MenuEvent, MouseEvent, MoveEvent, StatusEvent, TimerEvent, ValueEvent
Design objects	Menu, PopUpMenu, UIObject
Display managers	Application, Form, Report, TableView
Data types	AnyType, Array, Binary, Currency, Date, DateTime, DynArray, Graphic, Logical, LongInt, Memo, Number, OLE (object linking and embedding), Point, SmallInt, String, Time
Data model objects	Database, Query, Table, TCursor
System data objects	DDE (dynamic data exchange), FileSystem, Library, Session, System, TextStream

what happened (e.g., which mouse button or which key was pressed to elicit the action), and why the action happened (e.g., did the user do something or was the event generated from within ObjectPAL?). The code is the ObjectPAL method for extracting the data.

The event object type is the basis for all other object types in the events category. The methods defined for the event type are inherited by all of the derived object types. You cannot create new event types, nor can you change the method in the event object. You can, however, read and change event information. Every event generates an information packet about itself. The packet is of the event type as shown in the following example:

```
method arrive(var eventInfo MoveEvent)
; body of method goes here
endMethod
```

The information packet for the method arrive is stored in the variable eventInfo of type MoveEvent. Information in the eventInfo variable can be manipulated using the methods listed in Table 1.5.

Design Objects. *Design objects* (e.g., see Table 1.6) contain the code that executes in response to events. There are three categories of design object: Menus, PopUpMenus, and UIObjects. The UIObjects are used to create the user interface. UIObjects are the only objects in the ObjectPAL language that allow the developer to add custom methods. They include the buttons, boxes, bitmaps, table frames, and other objects in a form, including the form itself, with which the user interacts.

TABLE 1.5   ObjectPAL Events

Event type	Description
ActionEvent	This event type is generated when tables are being edited or navigated. In addition to the base set of Event methods, the actionClass, id, and setId methods are built into the ActionEvent type.
ErrorEvent	This event type is generated when an error occurs in an ObjectPAL application. ErrorEvent overloads the reason and setReason methods.
Event	This is the base event type. Event establishes the common methods for all other event types. These methods are errorCode, getTarget, isFirstTime, isPrefilter, isTargetSelf, reason, setErrorCode, and setReason.
KeyEvent	KeyEvents are generated when a keyboard action occurs. In addition to the base event methods, KeyEvent also has the char, charAnsiCode, isAltKeyDown, isControlKeyDown, isFormUI, isShiftKeyDown, setAltKeyDown, setChar, setControlKeyDown, setShiftKeyDown, setVChar, setVCharCode, vChar, and vCharCode.
MenuEvent	MenuEvents are generated when a user chooses an item from a menu. In addition to the base event methods, MenuEvent has the data, isFormUI, menChoice, setData, and setId. It has also overloaded the id and SetReason methods.
MouseEvent	A MouseEvent is generated whenever a mouse is clicked or moved over an object. The built-in methods for MouseEvent are getMousePosition, getObjectHit, isControlKeyDown, isFromUI, isInside, isLeftDown, isMiddleDown, isRightDown, isControlKeyDown, setInside, setLeftDown, setMiddleDown, setMousePosition, setRightDown, setShiftKeyDown, setX, setY, x, and y; in addition, the base Event methods are available.
MoveEvent	MoveEvents are generated as you move from one object to another in a form. The MoveEvent has a getDestination method and two overloaded Event methods—reason and setReason—as well as the remaining Event methods.
StatusEvent	StatusEvents control the messages that appear in the status bar. The methods setStatusValue and statusValue, the two overloaded methods reason and setReason, and the basic Event methods are built into the StatusEvent.
TimerEvent	TimerEvent actions are generated in response to setTimer, killTimer, and action methods of the UIObject type. It uses the base Event methods in response to these events.
ValueEvent	ValueEvents are generated when the value of a field is modified. The base Event methods are supplemented by a newValue and setNewValue method for this event type.

TABLE 1.6   ObjectPAL Design Objects

Object	Description
Menu	A menu object is a list of items displayed in the application menu bar. The built-in methods for the menu object are addArray, addBreak, addPopUp, addStaticText, addText, contains, count, empty, getMenuChoiceAttribute, getMenuChoiceAttributeByID, hasMenuChoiceAttribute, remove, removeMenusetMenuChoiceAttribute, setMenuChoiceAttributeById, and show.
PopUpMenu	A PopUpMenu is a vertical list of items that is displayed in response to an Event (usually a mouse click). A PopUpMenu includes the methods defined for the Menu type.
UIObject	UIObjects create the user interface for an application; every object the user interacts with is a UIObject. Only UIObjects have built-in methods (the form is a separate type, but also behaves as a UIObject in that methods can be attached to the form and the form reacts to events). The different UIObjects are the bitmap, box, button, crosstab, ellipse, field object, form, graph, line, multi-record object, OLE object, page, record object, table frame, and text box.
	The built-in methods of the UIObject are action, atFirst, atLast, attach, broadCastAction, cancelEdit, convertPointWithRespectTo, copyFromArray, copyToArray, create, currRecord, delete, deleteRecord, edit, empty, end, endEdit, enumFieldNames, enumLocks, enumObjectNames, enumSource, enumSourceToFile, enumUIClasses, enumUIObjectNames, enumUIObjectProperties, execMethod, getBoundingBox, getPosition, getProperty, getPropertyAsString, getRGB, hasMouse, home, insertAfterRecord, insertBeforeRecord, insertRecord, isContainerValid, isEdit, isEmpty, isLastMouseClickedValid, isLastMouseRightClickedValid, isRecordDeleted, keyChar, keyPhysical, killTimer, locate, locateNext, locateNextPattern, locatePattern, locatePrior, locatePriorPattern, lockRecord, lockStatus, menuAction, mouseClick, mouseDouble, mouseDown, mouseEnter, mouseExit, mouseMove, mouseRightDouble, mouseRightDown, mouseRightUp, mouseUp, moveTo, moveToRecNo, moveToRecord, nextRecord, nFields, nKeyFields, nRecords, pixelsToTwips, postAction, postRecord, priorRecord, pushButton, recordStatus, resync, rgb, setFilter, setPosition, setProperty, setTimer, skip, switchIndex, twipsToPixels, unDeleteRecord, unlockRecord, view, wasLastClicked, and wasLastRightClicked.

TABLE 1.7   ObjectPAL Display Managers

Object	Description
Application	An `Application` variable provides a handle for working with the `Desktop` window of the current Paradox application. The Application type includes methods defined for the `Form` type.
Form	The `Form` type is the base type from which the other display manager types are derived. The methods built into the `Form` type are `action, attach, bringToTop, close, create, delayScreenUpdates, design, disableBreakMessage, dmAddTable, dmGet, dmHasTable, dmPut, dmRemoveTable, enumSource, enumSourceToFile, enumTableLinks, enumUIObjectNames, enumUIObjectProperties, formCaller, formReturn, getPosition, getTitle, hide, hideSpeedBar, isMaximized, isMinimized, isSpeedBarShowing, isVisible, keyChar, keyPhysical, load, maximize, menuAction, methodDelete, methodGet, methodSet, minimize, mouseDouble, mouseDown, mouseEnter, mouseExit, mouseMove, mouseRightDouble, mouseRightDown, mouseRightUp, mouseUp, moveToPage, open, openAsDialog, postAction, run, save, setPosition, setTitle, show, showSpeedBar, wait, windowClientHandle,` and `windowHandle`. In addition, custom methods can be attached to the form.
Report	The `Report` type provides a handle to a report. `Report` methods control the window's size, position, and appearance, and to view and print the report. The `Report` type includes several methods defined for the `Form` type. Custom methods cannot be attached to a report. Methods available for the `Report` type include `attach, close, currentPage, design, enumUIObjectNames, enumUIObjectProperties, load, moveToPage, open, print,` and `run`.
TableView	A `TableView` object displays table data. `TableView` methods are a subset of the methods for the `Form` type. `TableView` methods include `action, close, open,` and `wait`.

Display managers. *Display managers* (e.g., see Table 1.7) are applications, forms, reports, and table views that display data. Users control the size, shape, position, and appearance of these objects.

Data types. Using the basic data types shown in Table 1.4, variables can be declared to store and manipulate the data. ObjectPAL supports the data formats available for development shown in Table 1.8.

Data model objects. *Data model objects* handle data stored in tables. The `Table`, `Query`, and `TCursor` types access and manipulate the data; the database type handles collections of tables. Data model

TABLE 1.8   ObjectPAL Data Types

Object	Description
AnyType	A data type used for situations in which the actual data type cannot be determined until the method executes
Array	An indexed collection of data
Binary	Machine-readable data
Currency	Used to manipulate currency values
Date	Calendar data
DateTime	Calendar and clock data combined
DynArray	A dynamic array
Graphic	A bitmap image
Logical	True or false
LongInt	Used to represent relatively large integer values
Memo	Holds lots of text
Number	Floating-point values
OLE	Object linking and embedding protocol for assessing data in another application without opening that application
Point	Information about a location on the screen
Record	A user-defined structure
SmallInt	Used to represent relatively small integer values
String	Letters
Time	Clock data

objects which provide access to and information about data stored in tables are shown in Table 1.9.

System data objects. The *system data objects* store and access data about a user's Windows environment, workstation setting, file directories, and network information. These objects are listed in Table 1.10.

ObjectPAL methods can address components at every level, binding them together to create graphical, event-driven applications as shown in Fig. 1.5.

TABLE 1.9   ObjectPAL Data Model Objects

Object	Description
Database	A collection of tables. In Paradox, a database and a directory are synonymous.
Query	A query variable represents a *query by example* (QBE) query. Methods associated with the query data type include `executeQBEfile`, `executeQBE`, `is assigned`, `writeQBE`, and `endquery`.
Table	A `Table` variable describes a table. It does not point to data; rather, it allows you to perform table-level actions (add, copy, create, sort, index, set filters, etc.) and specify table attributes (filters, indexes, access rights, etc.) prior to opening a table.
TCursor	A `TCursor` is a pointer to table data. It allows you to modify and manipulate data at the table, record, and field level.

TABLE 1.10   ObjectPAL Data Objects

Object	Description
DDE	A windows protocol for DDE between applications.
FileSystem	A `FileSystem` variable allows access to file data and information about files, drives, and directories.
Library	A file that stores custom methods, procedures, variables, constants, and user-defined data types.
Session	A session variable represents a channel to the Paradox database engine. Multiple sessions can be used within ObjectPAL to manage session-specific attributes such as retry periods, handling of blank values, and wildcards.
System	An object type for methods which do not fit in the other types. These methods include `enumFontsToTable`, `readEnvironmentString`, and `SysInfo`, which allow the application to determine information about the system it is running on.
TextStream	A sequence of ANSI characters (including carriage returns and line feeds) read from or written to a text file.

Events that trigger methods
(ActionEvent, ErrorEvent, Event, KeyEvent, MenuEvent,
MouseEvent, Status Event, TimerEvent, ValueEvent)

Design Objects that create the user interface
(Bitmap, Rectangle, Ellipse, Menu, Buton, Table Frame)

Display managers that control data selection and display
(Table View, Form, Report, Applications)

Data Types
(AnyType, Array, Binary, Currency, Date, DateTime,
DynArray, Graphic, Logica;, Longint, Memo, Number, OLE,
Point, SmallInt, String, Time)

Data Model Objects
(Query, TCursor, Table, Database)

System Data Objects for non-table data
(DDE, FileSystem, Library, Session, System, TextStream)

Figure 1.5   Components of an ObjectPAL application.

2

The Client/Server
Computing Environment

The development of a client/server system involves defining the client/server architecture and then integrating this architecture with other system architectures and technologies that are vital to client/server implementation. In this chapter, we will review each element of the client/server computing environment: resource sharing, distributed processing, relational database, network connectivity, and network management issues. In addition, we will summarize the role of SQL as an essential link in client/server computing and present an overview of the Open Systems Interconnection (OSI) standards for network development.

Client/Server Architecture

The architecture of a client/server system is distinguished by the incorporation of intelligent user workstations as active platforms and the interoperability between platforms and software. The client/server architecture involves multiple computers connected in a network. The computers that process applications and request services from another computer are called *clients*. The computer designed to process the database is called the *server*. All users have their own computers to process applications. The client computers can be mainframes, minicomputers, or microcomputers. Because of cost advantages, however, microcomputers are generally selected to act as clients. Likewise, the server is most often a microcomputer, but a mainframe or minicomputer may be used when greater power is required. In a database environment, the clients may communicate with the server by means of programming interfaces called *middleware*. These interfaces provide connectivity between applications and databases.

Figure 2.1 shows a single server, but the client/server architecture may include more than one server. In this event, however, each server must process a different database or provide a unique service. (*Note:* An architecture using two or more servers to process the same database is not considered to be a client/server system, but rather a distributed database system.)

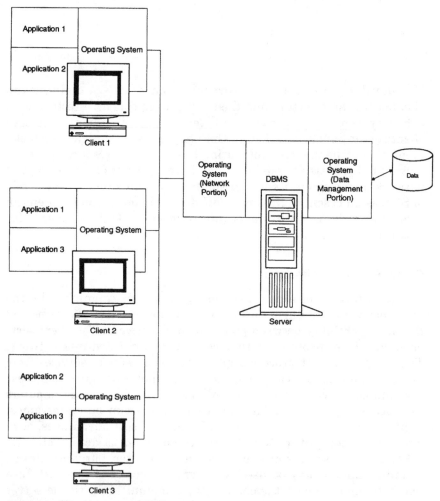

Figure 2.1   Client/server architecture.

TABLE 2.1   Roles for Client and Server Computers

Client functions	Server functions
Manage the user interface	Accept database requests from clients
Accept data from the user	Process database requests
Process application logic	Format results and transmit to client
Generate database requests	Perform integrity checking
Transmit database requests to server	Maintain database overhead data
	Provide concurrent access control
Receive results from server	Perform recovery
Format results	Optimize query and update processing

Table 2.1 summarizes the designated roles for computers in the client/server system.

The client

As noted, the client runs the programs that enable the user to formulate requests for services and passes the requests to the server. Computing done by the client is called *front-end processing*. The front-end processor handles all the functions related to presenting, manipulating, and displaying data.

The client *software* consists of the network interface software, the application programs supporting the user requirements, and utilities which utilize the network capabilities [e.g., electronic mail (e-mail), groupware]. The network interface software provides the functions that are described elsewhere in this chapter under the section heading OSI model. Applications software performs specific tasks such as word processing, spreadsheet, and database query generation. Utility software generally performs a standard task that is required by almost every network user.

The server

Computing performed at the server is called *back-end processing*. The *back-end hardware* is a computer that manages the data resources and performs the database engine functions such as storing, manipulating, and protecting data. In a mainframe environment, a *back-end network* provides the connection of mainframe computers to mass storage devices, controllers, and file servers. The identification, evaluation, and selection of the appropriate server platform must take into consideration the services to be provided by the server. For example, a database server may require a fast processing capability, rapid disk access, and possibly fault tolerance capabilities to ensure satisfactory network performance. Other network services that may need to be addressed are requirements for communications, applications, file access, and compact-disc read-only-memory (CD-ROM) services. The list of potential services which may be provided will continue to grow as new applications of technology become generally available.

Server *software* includes both the network software compliant with the OSI or other network architecture and the applications or services software provided by the server to the clients on the network.

Middleware

Middleware is a layer of software that shields applications developers from different communications protocols, operating systems, and database management systems. It provides the foundation for new applications that can coexist with legacy applications.

There are several types of middleware. They include applications programming interfaces (APIs), remote procedure calls (RPCs), network messaging, database access, and computer-aided software engineering (CASE) tools.

Since a client/server system requires the integration of various architectural components and technologies, applications programming can be quite complex. The selection of appropriate middleware can eliminate the need for programmers to write code for each individual protocol and operating system.

Resource-Sharing Architecture

The architecture of a resource-sharing system (see Fig. 2.2) differs from the architecture of a client/server system in that the database management system (DBMS) is on the local computers. Thus, special considerations must be given to integrating these two architectural concepts. In resource sharing, the DBMS on each user's computer must send requests to the operating system on the file server. In a client/server system, the request would simply be processed using the appropriate SQL command. Since the DBMS in the resource sharing architecture is on the local computer, the software needed to process SQL or any similar language is not available on the file server. Therefore, to access the data on another computer, the entire file (and possibly the associated index files) must be passed through the server.

A negative aspect of the resource-sharing architecture is that a large portion of the database must be locked while a user request is

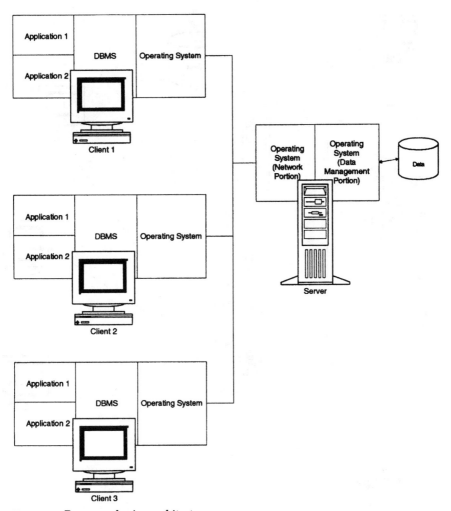

Figure 2.2   Resource-sharing architecture.

being processed. This reduces throughput, rendering the architecture incompatible with transaction processing. On the positive side, the query processing of downloaded data can be facilitated by designating a server that downloads large sections of data that does not have to be updated or returned to the database. This approach to resource sharing from downloaded data is effective for performing query and reporting functions. The use of resource sharing for processing downloaded data with a mainframe as a file server is shown in Fig. 2.3.

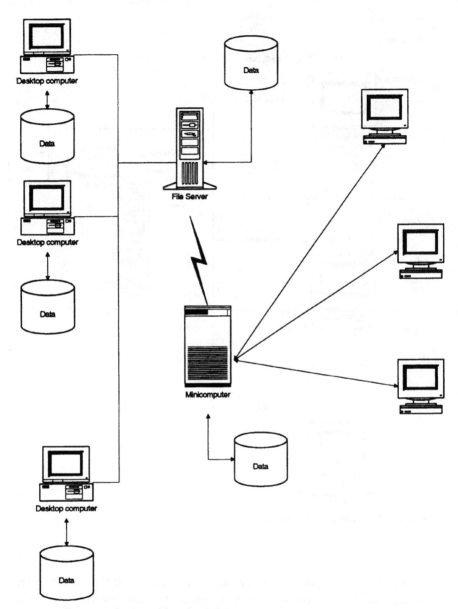

Figure 2.3   Resource sharing of downloaded data.

Distributed Database Architecture

Distributed database processing involves the execution of transactions and the updating of data across two or more geographically separated computers.

The hardware nodes in a distributed database system may be homogeneous or heterogeneous. The software required includes the *distributed database management system* (DDBMS), which consists of the collection of distributed transaction and database managers that reside at each node; a *distributed transaction manager* that receives processing requests from query or transaction programs and translates them into actions for the database managers; and a *database manager* that retrieves and updates data according to the action command.

Data in a distributed database system may be nonreplicated, partially replicated, or fully replicated. *Nonreplicated data* means that only one copy of each data item exists. These data items reside only at their assigned node. Access to these data must be obtained from that node.

Several types of procedures must be considered in distributed database processing. Procedures that grant processing rights define which nodes have access to the data. Procedures that concern currency are necessary to avoid processing of outdated data. Control procedures are needed to resolve problems that may arise from conflicting processing requests.

Figure 2.4 illustrates a typical distributed database system.

Distributing applications

The distributing of applications via client/server systems involves special consideration in four specific areas: parallel application processing; database integrity and constraint checking; triggers; and concurrent processing control, and recovery.

Parallel processing. The client/server architecture enables client computers to process applications in parallel while the server processes database requests. Although the client computers on the network must wait for the server to process each database query, they do not have to wait for each other to process applications. Figure 2.5 shows the processing of multiple client computers and one server.

Database integrity and constraint checking. To ensure database integrity, the data must be checked during the processing operations. The

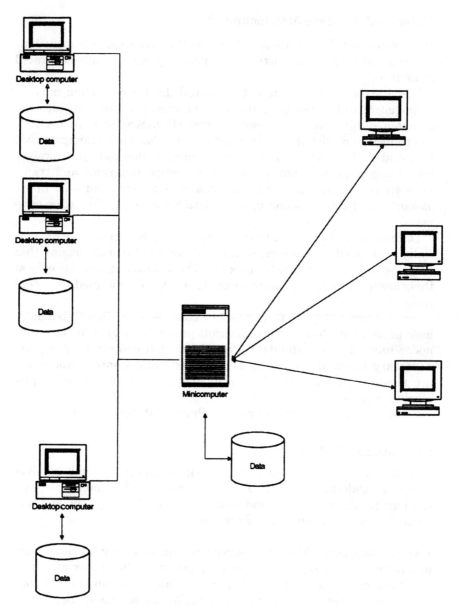

Figure 2.4 Distributed database architecture.

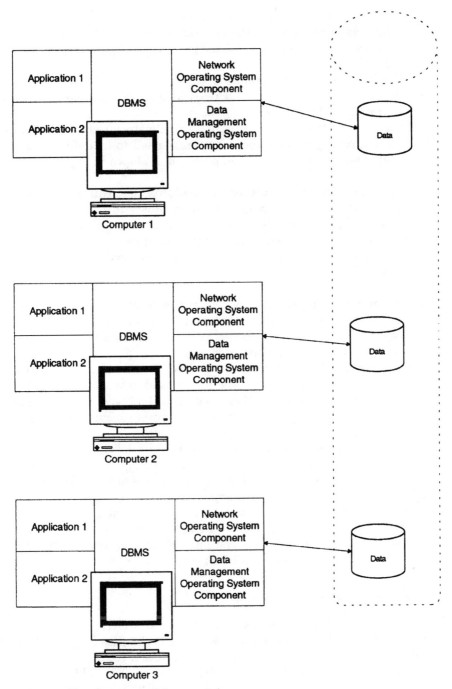

Figure 2.5 Client/server parallel processing.

checking functions may be performed by either clients or the server. Since database processing in the client/server architecture is consolidated on a single computer, database integrity and constraint checking is greatly facilitated.

If the integrity and constraints are checked by the client computers, the checking logic must be included in every application program as illustrated in Fig. 2.6.

If the server performs the integrity and constraint checking functions, the integrity factors and constraints need to be defined, verified, and validated in a centralized program as shown in Fig. 2.7.

Triggers. *Triggers* refer to those procedures that can be initiated automatically when a specified condition exists in the data of the database. A trigger code written for an application informs the DBMS of the conditions under which the trigger shall be invoked. The trigger is a function of the DBMS and so, in a client/server environment, resides on the server.

Concurrent processing control, backup, and recovery. Concurrent processing control must be exercised to protect against lost updates and inconsistent reads. This may be accomplished in either of two ways: (1) implicit locking and (2) delayed locking.

To invoke implicit lock control, the DBMS must be able to place locks on each DBMS command. The lock is held until the command is given to release the lock. Implicit locks can, however, create severe delays if the DBMS does not address problems of concurrent requests that frequently occur in multiuser environments.

Control via delayed locking is accomplished by delaying the locking function as long as possible. This reduces the waiting time required, but also has a negative effect. The logic is more complicated than the logic of implicit lock control, placing a greater processing burden on the application programmer or the client portion of the DBMS.

When failures occur, the server DBMS must be able to perform recovery functions to place the system back into an error-free state from which normal operations can be resumed.

Relational Database Architecture

A *relational database* is defined as a database in which the individual files, termed *relations,* hold data in the form of flat files or tables. The table must contain only one type of record. Each record has a fixed number of fields, all of which are explicitly named. The fields within a

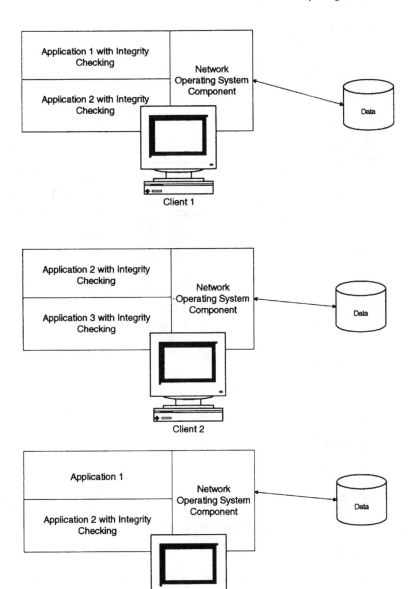

Figure 2.6 Integrity and constraint checking by client computers.

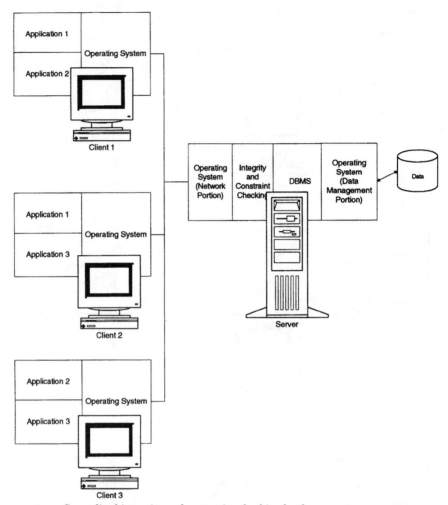

Figure 2.7 Centralized integrity and constraint checking by the server.

table are distinct, and repeating groups are not allowed. There are no duplicate records and no predetermined sequence of records.

In the construction of a relational database, it is necessary to give careful consideration to the contents of relations and the inherent relationships between attributes (fields) of a record.

The fundamental operations on a relational database are selection, projection, join, and division. Selection produces a new table containing the same number of columns as the original relation, but the rows will contain those of the original relation that satisfy some specified criteria. The projection operation specifies columns to be selected. The resulting table thus contains only a subset of the columns of the original table. If two rows differ in the columns deleted by the projection, only one record will be carried forward to the new relation. The join operation combines information from two or more tables. A common field in the two tables is used as the basis of the combination of records. Records with equal values in the common field are concatenated in the resulting relation.

Relational database implementation tasks

The tasks involved in implementing a relational database are divided into three groups: (1) tasks required to define the structure of the database to the DBMS, (2) tasks required to allocate the database to physical storage media, and (3) tasks required to create database data. The means by which these tasks are performed depends on the DBMS product used.

Various DBMS products provide utilities for defining the database structure that use a specified data definition language (DDL). Provisions are included with some DBMS products for allocating the database to physical media once the database has been defined to the DBMS. Depending on the nature of application processing, the data may be located on designated tables or on the same disk. Some DBMS products focus on the creation of database data.

As previously stated, the database definition, storage allocation, and data creation procedures will depend on the applications requirements and the features of the particular DBMS product selected.

Relational data manipulation

To implement applications, a language for expressing process logic is required. There are four categories of relational data manipulation language:

Relational algebra, which is a language that provides a set of operators for manipulating relations in a relational database.

Relational calculus, a language in which a user specifies the set of results required from the manipulation of the data in a relational database.

Transform-oriented languages, which constitute a class of nonprocedural languages that transform input data expressed as relations into results expressed as a single relation. SQL is a transform-oriented language.

Graphical-oriented systems, which provide the user with a picture of the structure of a relation. Borland's Paradox and IBM's QBE (query by example) are examples.

Users can interface with a relational database in several ways. Some DBMS products include tools for generating forms and provide for the processing of the forms and reports. Query languages also provide an interface. They perform both query and update functions. The most important query language, which was discussed earlier in this chapter, is SQL. A third means of interfacing with the relational database is via applications program.

Object-Oriented Database Management Systems

Relational database technology is based on a well-articulated mathematical model based on uniform data structures and relatively simple relationships. The complex data structures associated with today's office information systems, however, may include such diverse components as text, graphics, voice, and video. These data are *not* uniformly structured, making their incorporation into traditional relational DBMSs difficult. Object-oriented databases have recently been introduced to solve such functions as document management, workflow management, and groupware processes.

Numerous vendors have object-oriented database management systems (OODBMSs) on the market. Included in this market are Ontos, Object Design, Objectivity, Versant Object Technology, Servio Logic Corp., and Matisse. In addition, many systems are being introduced that combine the relational and object models to create either hybrid systems or extended relational systems.

Hybrid systems

Hybrid database systems place an object-oriented front end on top of a relational database kernel. The front end decomposes the application objects and stores them in a relational table. When needed, the objects are then recomposed and presented to the user. This approach is effective from the object-oriented development point of view, but does impose performance overhead. A typical hybrid system is Hewlett Packard's OpenODB.

Extended relational systems

Extensions to the relational model are being made by numerous vendors. These extensions include storage of complex data types in relational tables, stored procedures, triggers, and binary large objects (BLOBs). The extensions of SQL now being considered in the SQL3 standards will include further support for objects. These will likely include support of user-defined data types and nested tables. Vendors providing object extensions to the relational model include Sybase, Informix, Oracle, and Borland.

SQL: An Essential Link

SQL provides an essential link in the integrated client/server architecture discussed in the preceding paragraphs. It was developed by IBM in the mid-1970s under the name SEQUEL. It was renamed SQL in 1980. SQL has been endorsed as the recognized industry standard for manipulating databases by the American Standards Institute (ANSI). It is the data access language used by many database management system (DBMS) products.

SQL allows users to run queries on relational table data, create new tables, access existing remote tables, manipulate data, create applications to access SQL data, run SQL statements, handle errors, and access multiple servers. The SQL database servers are multiuser relational database management systems (RDBMSs).

SQL commands can be used interactively as a query language or embedded in applications programs. In performing a query, SQL accepts one or more relations as input and produces a single relation as output. The result is a table or flat file (i.e., a collection of records of the same type which do not contain repeating groups). In querying multiple tables, the tables are joined by SQL. Provisions are included in SQL for inserting new data into a table, deleting data from a table, or modifying table data.

Server Data Management Facilities

Server data management encompasses facilities that enable data to be accessed from any node in the network and to ensure privacy, recovery, and integrity in a multiuser environment. As previously noted, the essential access link in client/server computing is SQL, a high-level, nonprocedural database language. Numerous back-end servers and DBMSs have been developed that support SQL. These include the products described below and on the following pages.

DB2

DB2 is a RDBMS developed by IBM. It uses SQL to perform all database operations: data definition, data access, data manipulation, and authorization functions. SQL statements are entered by a user at a client node or embedded in applications.

DB2 constructs include tables, views, table spaces, indexes, index space, databases, and storage groups. The RDBMS provides facilities that allow users to dynamically create and modify these constructs. DB2 also includes concurrent processing facilities to control and limit interference, backup and recovery facilities, and security facilities.

Concurrent processing is accomplished via *locks*. When an application reads database data, DB2 acquires a shared lock on the data that allows other applications to read the same data. If an application needs to modify data, DB2 places an exclusive lock on the data to prevent other applications from accessing the data. DB2 also offers options regarding the level or locksize.

All database changes are stored and checked periodically by DB2. All changes residing in system buffers are written to the database, and a change record is logged. Recovery from a system failure is accomplished by applying all images created since the most recent changes written to the log. DB2 includes utility programs for re-creating the database from backup copies. This utility includes an option that allows users to make backup copies of only those pages in a table space that have been modified since the last backup was performed.

DB2 also includes security provisions to protect the database.

Borland object component architecture (BOCA)

BOCA establishes a client/server foundation that takes into consideration both development tools and database management tools. It brings together an array of object-oriented tools, middleware, and database server technologies to provide client/server solutions. The components of the architecture are

Advanced object-oriented tools. Borland has created a broad spectrum of tightly integrated, object-oriented tools that take full advantage of the client/server revolution. Borland C++. Turbo Pascal, Paradox, dBase, Quattro Pro, and Object Vision are all built using object-oriented methodologies.

IDAPI. IDAPI (integrated database application programming interface) is Borland's connectivity solution. IDAPI enables developers to create database applications more productively and allows end users to access data stored in multiple formats on a wide variety of hardware and operating systems platforms and network environments.

InterBase.   InterBase is a distributed SQL database server that lets each database system query and return information to any other InterBase server. InterBase's versioning architecture represents the third wave of relational systems technology. The versioning engine enables InterBase to support both high transaction processing and decision support transaction with minimized locking.

Borland's object orientation enables developers to build complex client/server systems by constructing modular application components that can be easily developed, tested, maintained, and enhanced and readily assembled into complex application suites. The object-oriented development concepts of ObjectPAL and C++ also provide for end-user productivity. The programming languages enable end-user applications to be constructed with reusable object components. The applications constructed from similar components can be easily integrated to allow users to exchange departmental and enterprise resources such as data, forms, reports, spreadsheets, and graphics among their desktop applications. To support the applications development effort, Borland has created an *object-oriented user interface* (OOUI).

Gupta SQL system

The Gupta SQL system includes Gupta Quest, Gupta SQL Windows, Gupta SQLBase, and Gupta SQLNetwork.

Gupta Quest is a graphical data access and reporting tool for Windows, targeted specifically for SQL databases. *Gupta SQLWindows* is a client/server application system for Windows featuring collaborative programming and object orientation.

Gupta SQLBase is a high-performance SQL DBMS, scalable from laptops to LAN servers.

Gupta SQLNetwork provides connectivity software from graphical PC clients to LAN database servers and enterprise SQL databases. It supports IBM DB2 Database Manager and AS/400, Oracle, Gupta SQLBase Server, Microsoft and Sybase SQL Server, Informix, Cincom Supra, and HP ALLBASE/SQL.

Informix SQL server family

Informix offers several products to answer specific client/server needs. They include Informix-On-Line, Informix TP/XA, Informix-Star, Informix On-Line/Optical, and Informix On-Line Workstation Manual.

Informix-On-Line is an *on-line transaction-processing* (OLTP) database server with high-availability, data integrity, and multimedia data management capabilities. It achieves its high performance by establishing efficient data storage methods for fast data access, buffering data in memory to minimize disk access, utilizing multiprocessor features to enable simultaneous access by different processors, and determining the most efficient search strategy automatically.

Informix-TP/XA links On-Line to transaction managers to support those transactions involving multiple databases and perhaps multiple DBMSs from different vendors. Informix is the first RDBMS to provide this standards-based interface to X/Open XA-compliant transaction managers.

Informix-STAR is the distributed, client/server database product for On-Line that provides optimized performance with minimal network traffic, location transparency, and high reliability for manipulating multiple databases at different locations.

Informix-On-Line/Optical is an add-on product for On-Line users who want mass storage capabilities of optical devices for their database system. It allows users to store BLOBs on write-once read-many (WORM) optical subsystems. Users must have On-Line/Optical, On-Line, and an optical subsystem. Without the On-Line/Optical product, users can still manipulate BLOBs with On-Line on magnetic storage devices.

Informix-On-Line Workstation Manual is a graphical version of the On-Line Administrator's Manual. The workstation manual has the same technical content as the hard-copy version, but it is structured in a windowed, point-and-click graphical interface with key-word cross-references. This enables the user to access the information needed in one window while configuring, monitoring, or tuning On-Line in another.

Microsoft SQL server family

The products offered as part of the Microsoft SQL Server family include Microsoft SQL Server for Windows NT, Microsoft SQL Administrator for Windows, Microsoft SQL Bridge, and Microsoft SQL Server Programmer's Toolkits.

Microsoft SQL Server for Windows NT is designed to manage large databases for mission-critical applications and meet the demands of networked client/server applications.

Microsoft SQL Administrator for Windows allows network management with a graphical server administration tool for Windows- and OS/2-based systems.

Microsoft SQL Bridge provides a protocol gateway between Microsoft SQL Server environments and Sybase SQL Server environments.

Microsoft SQL Programmer's Toolkits offer flexibility in developing client/server applications that deliver critical corporate information to Windows-, MS-DOS-, and OS/2-based desktop systems using C, Visual Basic, and COBOL programming languages.

Oracle RDBMS

The Oracle RDBMS provides operations, administration, and management facilities that mission-critical, enterprise-scale applications require. With Oracle RDBMS's distributed database and gateway capabilities, users can transparently integrate the enterprise's new and legacy data, systems, and applications. Oracle is grouped into seven packages to enable customers to acquire only the functionality their applications need: (1) the standard Oracle package, (2) the procedural option package, (3) the distributed object package, (4) the parallel server option package, and (5) the open gateway package.

The *Standard Oracle* package provides the functionality and performance required to tackle a broad range of mission-critical on-line data-processing (OLDP) and decision support applications. The standard package includes all the features of the other six packages, plus the following features that are unique to the Standard Oracle package.

The *procedural option* for Oracle provides several capabilities that enable the database server to be an active component of the applications environment. The procedural option is well suited for applications with advanced requirements and complex business rules to enforce. It optionally includes the ability to use programming language/SQL (PL/SQL) procedures within the Oracle server, with stored procedures and functions, procedure packages, database triggers, lock manager package, and database alerts. It also permits "anonymous" PL/SQL procedures to be submitted interactively and from 3GL (third-generation language) programs.

The *distributed option* allows a physically distributed database to be treated as a single logical database. Applications which require updating data on multiple locations may benefit from the distributed option. The features of this option include distributed updates, transaction processing (TP) monitor (XA) interface, transparent two-phase commit, remote procedure calls (RPCs), table replication (snapshots), and an Oracle Mail interface. The query capability and global database names are included with the Standard Oracle server.

The *parallel server option* provides support for multiple nodes of loosely coupled systems to concurrently access a single database for OLTP and decision support. The parallel server delivers significant benefits in the areas of high performance, expandability, high availability, and database consolidations. The parallel server option includes parallel cache management and all other features required for loosely coupled and massively parallel platforms.

The *Oracle open gateway package* provides programmable and transparent access to data in non-Oracle data managers, file systems, applications, and systems of all sorts. Oracle Corporation uses open gateway technology to provide SQL connect gateways to many popular database systems and file systems for transparent SQL access.

For target data managers for which no SQL connect product is available, the *Oracle Open Gateway Developer's Kit* can facilitate the integration of open-systems-based applications with legacy systems, data, and applications.

For organizations desiring access controls based on the sensitivity or classification of data, *Trusted Oracle* includes all the features of Oracle 7, along with multilevel security.

Sybase SQL server family

The Sybase client/server architecture consists of three product families: Sybase SQL server, Sybase SQL life-cycle tools, and Sybase open interoperability products.

The *Sybase SQL Server* is an RDBMS for on-line applications. It provides subsecond response times, low-cost-per-user operation, and high availability. The *SQL Server Intelligent Data Dictionary* is the repository for data definitions, business rules, reports, and configuration information.

Sybase SQL life-cycle tools provide a means to quickly prototype, build, and maintain on-line applications that model the business, enforce business rules, protect data integrity, and integrate existing applications with new data sources. They allow developers to work through the various stages of the SQL application life cycle. With Sybase tools, developers can use any combination of SQL, 3GLs, 4GLs, multimedia, and object-oriented tools to build on-line systems.

Sybase's interoperability strategy provides both extensive toolkits for developing client and server applications as well as turn-key gateways to the most popular RDBMSs. This strategy makes it possible for a complex computing environment of heterogeneous hardware, operating systems, networks, databases, and applications to work together.

OSI Model

To enable the devices on a network to communicate over different communications links, a uniform set of protocols must be constructed.

The *open systems interconnection* (OSI) model provides the basis for considerable independence between the various and complicated operations of data communications. The model divides the work to be performed into tasks arranged sequentially in layers. At each level the process communicates with its corresponding layer in the receiving host by accepting messages from the layer that is above it, adding control information to the message and then passing the message to the layer immediately below. The process is reversed at the receiving end. Messages are received from the layer below, control information is stripped off, and the message is passed up to the next layer. The OSI layers are illustrated in Fig. 2.8.

The *physical layer* is the lowest level of the OSI model. It is concerned with the transmission of a raw bitstream. The layer uses error-detecting codes and host-to-host control messages to convert an unreliable transmission channel into a reliable one. This network layer, in a point-to-point network is primarily concerned with routing and congestion.

The *data-link layer* provides the basic packet delivery functions for the network. The final assembly on leaving packets and the first inspection on arriving packets is accomplished at this layer. It adds error correction on the leaving packets and validates checksum data on arriving packets.

The *network layer* is concerned primarily with the provision of services to establish a path, with a predictable quality of service, between open systems. It is responsible for routing datagrams hop by hop over a potentially complex network of individual links.

The *transport layer* is responsible for reliable delivery of the user messages from one computer to another, including the conversion of arbitrary-length messages to the datagrams which the network layer processes.

The *session layer* provides for connections between processes in different hosts. It includes those functions involved in establishing communications between two applications.

The *presentation layer* performs translations of data formats [e.g. translations between American Standard Code for Information Interchange (ASCII) and Extended Binary Coded Decimal Interchange Code (EBCDIC) encoding schemes]. It performs any conversions that may be required to render the data usable by the application layer. The presentation layer of network communications should not be confused with the frequently used term *presentation* in discussions concerning the presentation of data to the user. The presentation layer in the OSI model is a network communication layer and does not interface directly with a display device.

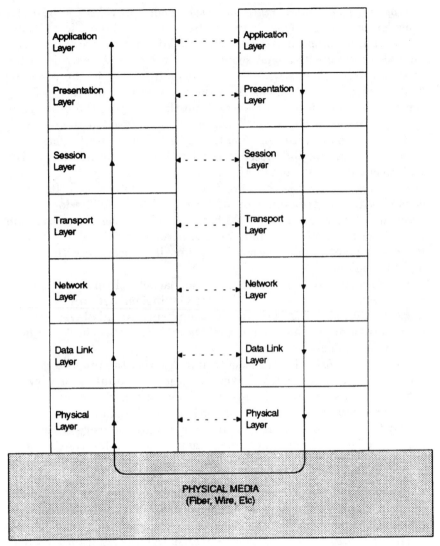

Figure 2.8 OSI seven-layer model.

The *application layer* provides a set of network services (file transfer, e-mail, etc.) to the applications program. *Application layer* is the generic term for all the software which performs a user-visible function.

Network Connectivity

The development of a client/server system also requires an understanding of a variety of network connectivity issues. These include issues pertaining to physical media, physical topologies, communications protocols, asynchronous communications services, internetworking, and local connectivity support.

Physical media

Physical media types are classified as follows: unshielded twisted pair (UTP), shielded twisted pair (STP), coaxial cable, and optical fiber.

Physical topologies

The basic physical topologies for network design are classified as follows:

Star topology, which provides a central hub through which all messages pass

Ring topology, in which all the nodes are connected together in a ring, with none having overall control of access to the network

Loop topology, in which all nodes are connected together in a ring but one of them controls the rest and determines which should use the communications channel

Bus topology, which provides a single communications circuit that is shared by every node, but the circuit is not joined together in a loop

Tree topology, in which the nodes are connected together by a branching communication channel

Communications protocols

Data communications protocols coordinate the exchange of information between different network devices. The following network protocols support the workgroup and enterprise model of client/server computing:

Xerox Network Systems (XNSs), designed to enable users to make use of a range of services on the network: e-mail, electronic document exchange, and remote printing of documents

Internetwork Datagraph Protocol (IDP), designed to perform packet-routing functions in the XNS

Routing Information Protocol (RIP), which uses IDP to exchange routing information between routers

Sequenced Packet Protocol (SPP), that establishes a virtual circuit between the sender and the receiver

Packet Exchange protocol (PEP), which provides a connectionless protocol for simple request/response-type communications between applications processes

Courier Protocol, designed to control the calling of remote procedures that are located and executed on remote computers

Novell NetWare Protocol (IPX/SPX), a modified version of the RIP used to query and maintain routing-information tables on clients and servers

Internetwork Packet Exchange (IPX), derived from IDP; provides a connectionless, unreliable, datagram service to clients and servers

Sequenced Packet Exchange (SPX), which provides a virtual circuit service between network nodes

NetWare Core Protocol (NCP), designed to interface with workstations that make requests for network services from NetWare file servers

Service Advertising Protocol (SAP), which enables servers to advertise their names and the type of services they provide

NetBIOS, a high-level application program interface that was designed to enable programmers to build network applications using IBM's PC Network

AppleTalk Protocol Suite, which enables users to share files across an AppleTalk network

Datagram Delivery Protocol (DDP), which serves as AppleTalk's network layer protocol

Transmission Control Protocol (TCP), which provides a reliable connection-oriented virtual circuit service for application processes to use for host-to-host communications

User Datagram Protocol (UDP), which provides application processes with an unreliable datagram protocol for the transport layer

Internet Protocol, which provides an unreliable, connectionless datagram service for switching data over packet-switched networks

Internet Control Message Protocol (ICMP), used to report errors that occur during the delivery of datagrams through the internet

Network asynchronous communications

The sharing of network resources is made possible through the use of asynchronous communication devices that enable users to share modems. The two basic methods used are parallel and serial communications. *Parallel communication* is a method in which each bit of a word is sent simultaneously on an individual wire. *Serial communica-*

tion is a method of information transfer in which each bit of a character is sent in sequence.

Parallel transmission requires eight wires to convey individual bytes and is therefore used mainly for transmission over short distances (e.g., for buses within a computer).

Serial transmission requires some means of converting individual bits of data to facilitate data transmission. The data is broken into packets by a universal synchronous receiver-transmitter (UART). Other facilities include the RS-232 connector and a modem. *The RS-232 connector* is a standard employed in serial connections for computers. The standard has four parts: electrical signal characteristics, interface mechanical characteristics, functional description of the signals, and a list of standard interface types. Modems are responsible for the conversion of data. A capability of the modem is to modulate the signals in different ways.

LAN communications

The basic requirements of asynchronous communications across a local network are the dial-in and dial-out capabilities of the modems.

Dial-in includes the capability to access file information or run applications. In dialing into the network, a startup session must exist on a local node. To implement the system, some type of remote-control software is needed for both clients and servers. Examples of such software applications are pcAnywhere IV, Carbon Copy, Triton's Co/Session, and Norton-Lambert's Close Up. A dedicated server may be used to enable multiple DOS (disk operating system) sessions through one dedicated PC. Novell's NetWare Access Server is an example. MicroDyne Corporation has released a dedicated 80386 Access Server that comes equipped with the necessary adapters and either four or eight modems.

Dial-out services are accomplished by either software solutions that make the modem a shared device, dedicated modem pooling servers, or devices that are shared modems attached as a network device. Products that support network dial-out services include

InstantCom Communications Server (ICS), a software-only package that allows users to share a modem attached to a workstation.

Novell's NetWare Asynchronous Communications Server (NACS), which allows users to share modems that are attached directly to NetWare.

Telebit Asynchronous Communications Server (TACS), which supports both NetBIOS and NetWare protocols.

Internetworking

The proliferation of client/server computing has given emphasis to the development of a computing infrastructure called *internetworking*. This concept encompasses the linking of local and enterprise networks through devices such as bridges, routers, and gateways. Internetworking devices that correspond with the various levels of the OSI model include

Repeaters: bidirectional devices that amplify or regenerate signals in a channel. The repeaters are spaced along long communications channels subject to excessive attenuation or interference.

Bridges: devices that provide connections between networks, particularly local area networks on a local basis.

Switches: devices that create virtual links between individual nodes on different segments and allow multiple simultaneous connections.

Routers: devices that handle specific network-layer protocols used by end nodes to communicate with one another.

Gateways: devices used to interface networks so that a terminal can communicate with a terminal or computer on another network.

Connectivity support

Connectivity support for both local area networks and wide area communications can be derived from commonly used sets of protocols. Two such protocols are Novell NetWare and Microsoft LAN Manager.

Novell NetWare provides support for DOS, OS/2, Macintosh, and UNIX workstations. DOS workstations can be run by using the open data-link interface (ODLI) architecture. OS/2 workstations are run using device drivers that perform functions such as interrupts, passing addresses, error detection, and data buffering. NetWare for Macintosh uses the AppleTalk Filing Protocol (AFP) to handle requests from the file server. NetWare NFS software is used to integrate UNIX workstations with the NetWare to support file sharing, implementation of a presentation-layer syntax, mounting of the NetWare file system, printing of queues and printers, file exchanges, and record locking. The LAN standards used to connect network devices to form a NetWare internetwork include Ethernet, Token Ring, ARCnet, and LocalTalk. The Novell NetWare suite include:

Internetwork Packet Exchange (IPX), provides workstations and servers with addressing and internetwork services.

Sequence Packet Exchange (SPX), a connection-oriented protocol that provides a reliable peer-to-peer data stream between communicating network applications.

NetWare Shell, which interacts with applications on the client workstations. It encapsulates the request and redirects it via the network to a NetWare server.

NetWare Core Protocol (NCP), which controls the interaction between the workstation and the file server. It establishes the connections between them and processes requests for services from the file server.

Open Data Link Interface (ODLI), where multiple protocol stacks can be used with one or more adapters in a workstation on the network.

Transmission Control Protocol (TCP), provides a routing capability that allows IP packets to be forwarded through an IP internet.

IP Tunneling, a service that enables NetWare IPX LANs to be linked together using an IP internetwork. The IP Tunnel module enables the network administrator to configure network peers.

Microsoft LAN Manager provides support for Microsoft's Windows, UNIX, and OS/2. It was designed to handle a variety of functions related to data security, file sharing, multitasking, common device drivers, file-size limits, limits on the total number of files, caching of disk data, virtual memory, and memory protection. The commonly used protocols used in Microsoft LAN communications are *NetBEUI,* which supports the NetBIOS interface standards; and *TCP/IP,* which supports all NDIS-compliant device drivers.

LAN Manager for UNIX runs on the UNIX host computer and permits DOS, or OS/2-based workstations to access files, applications. A number of manufacturers support LAN Manager for UNIX. These include Data General, Group Bull, Hewlett-Packard, NCR, Olivetti, Unisys, and Santa Cruz Operation SCO.

Network Management

The focus of network management is on administrative control of day-to-day operations such as backup, configuration, inventory, version control, software license metering, and virus detection.

The critical issues pertaining to *backup* are those related to the selection of backup hardware and software, location of backup data, frequency of backup, preservation of file attributes, and the restoration of files.

Configuration issues that must be addressed pertain to the selection of utilities to facilitate efficient network operations such as the installation of device drivers and protocols and the definition of abstract network resources such as shares, devices, queues, and services.

Automatic *inventory* software is used to determine the basic hardware, operating system, and network configuration of the clients on the network.

One of the most important issues that must be addressed is *version control and distribution.* Automatic software distribution is a rapidly growing area of network management concern. Several vendors provide software-distribution software.

Software license metering facilitates detection of unauthorized uses. This software monitors the number of users accessing a program simultaneously and determines whether the number of users exceeds the number of licenses purchased.

The methods used for *virus detection* include checks for changing file sizes, performing checksums, or changing system boot and program disk areas.

OSI network management

The OSI management model identifies five functional areas of network management:

Fault management to facilitate fault detection, diagnosis, correction, and administration

Configuration management to identify, configure, and control devices on the network

Performance management to evaluate the system's reliability and level of performance

Accounting management to track and to control the network resources

Security management to protect against unauthorized access and use of network resources

The OSI management model defines the relationships between managed objects (see Fig. 2.9). Each object performs a designated task and consists of a separate piece of software.

SNMP-based network management

The Simple Network Management Protocol (SNMP) model closely follows the OSI framework. The management information base (MIB) is

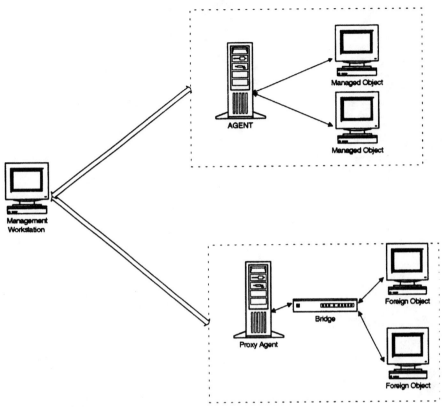

Figure 2.9 Relationship between managed objects.

the database of the objects to be managed. SNMP management tools include the *Carnegie-Mellon University* (CMU) *package*, which provides a command-line interface to Get and SetNMP MIB variables, and *VisiNet* from VisiSoft, which provides a graphical user interface.

3

Object-Oriented Client/Server Development Framework

A methodology for developing an object-oriented client/server system is outlined in this chapter. The approach to systems development is characterized by breaking down the work to be performed into four major functional areas:

Analysis

Design

Implement and test

Maintain

Each functional area is further broken down into phases that make up the development life cycle. The methodology for systems development outlined in this chapter and detailed in Part 2 provides step-by-step descriptions of the tasks to be performed for each phase. The phases of object-oriented client/server system development are illustrated in Fig. 3.1.

The life-cycle functions are preceded by a decision support activity triggered by the *project request,* which provides general information regarding the problem and need and includes preliminary estimates of costs and benefits.

Analysis

The analysis process is accomplished in three phases: *initial investigation, feasibility study,* and *requirements definition.* The process is

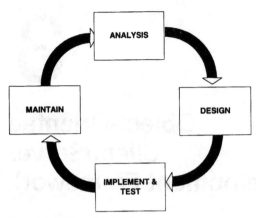

Figure 3.1 Life-cycle phases.

concerned with providing management with sufficient data to permit intelligent decision making regarding the economic justification and technical feasibility of developing and implementing the proposed project; and, with defining the functional, performance, environmental, and data requirements of the proposed system. The results of each analysis task and task step are recorded as they are completed. When all the tasks for a given phase have been completed and the results recorded, the document records are delivered to a project file and placed under configuration control. The process is illustrated in Fig. 3.2.

Initial investigation

The initial investigation allows management to estimate the potential of the proposed system in terms of costs and benefits. It provides a statement of existing problems, projects costs and schedules for development and operation of the proposed system, and produces a feasibility study work plan. The initial investigation report serves as the vehicle for communicating the preliminary assessment of the technical and economic impact of the proposed system. The initial investigation breaks down into eight major tasks:

Task 1: Assess project request.   The objective of this task is to assess the problem and need and validate that the costs and benefits indicated on the project request are realizable. The task steps are

- Assess timing of the proposed project to ensure that the development of the project will not be disruptive to the enterprise.

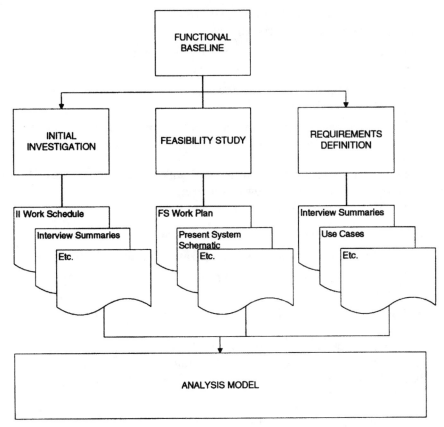

Figure 3.2 The analysis process.

- Assess potential conflicts which may adversely affect the successful implementation of the proposed system.
- Assess whether the project requested is compatible with and meets the plan and goals of the enterprise.

Task 2: Establish repository. The objective of this task is establish a repository for maintaining documentation and collected data. The task steps are

- Define acquisition functions for both internally and externally generated documents.
- Define procedures for cataloging, classifying, and indexing documents to be entered into the repository.

- Establish a plan for the physical organization and maintenance of items entered into the repository.

- Develop procedures for controlling the circulation of repository materials.

- Define procedures for the disposition of project materials at the completion of the project.

- Define change management procedures for incorporating changes to baseline documents and vendor supplied documents.

Task 3: Prepare to conduct initial investigation. The objective of this task is to schedule interviews and prepare materials to be used in conducting the interviews. The task steps are

- Establish schedules for conducting the interviews.

- Identify those individuals and organizational units to be interviewed.

- Formulate the questions to be asked in gathering information about the problem.

- List existing documentation from which data can be gleaned.

Task 4: Conduct user management interviews. The objective of this task is to gather information that will enable both data processing and user management to evaluate the costs and benefits of the proposed project. The task steps are

- Conduct initial investigation interviews.

- Document initial investigation interview responses.

- Collect supporting documentation.

- Review initial investigation interview summaries with respondent to ensure accuracy and correct representation.

Task 5: Analyze collected data. The objective of this task is to analyze the collected data in order to make preliminary determinations relative to the project costs and target schedules. The task steps are

- Analyze needs data.

- Analyze problem data.

- Analyze anticipated benefits.

Task 6: Prepare feasibility study work plan. The objective of this task is to prepare a plan for conducting a feasibility study. The task steps are

- Develop a work plan for reviewing the present system.

- Develop a work plan for determining preliminary requirements to the proposed system.

- Develop a work plan for identifying development alternatives.

- Develop a work plan for identifying technical support needs.

- Develop a work plan for conducting an economic evaluation of the proposed project.

Task 7: Prepare initial investigation report. The objective of this task is to prepare the initial investigation report for management review and approval to proceed. The content of the initial investigation report includes a management summary and a feasibility study work plan.

Task 8: Deliver initial investigation supporting documentation to repository. The objective of this task is to deliver the data collected during the initial investigation to the repository for indexing and maintenance. (*Note:* The project request is the first item delivered to the project repository.)

Feasibility study

The feasibility study is concerned with providing management with sufficient data to permit intelligent decision making regarding the economic justification and technical feasibility of the proposed project. The documentation focuses on defining the characteristics of the existing system and the requirements of the proposed system. The feasibility study breaks down into eight major tasks:

Task 1: Review initial investigation data. The objective of this task is to review the initial investigation data maintained in the repository. The task steps are

- Review initial investigation interview summaries.

- Review supporting documents and other exhibits collected during the initial investigation.

- Review the feasibility study work plan.

Task 2: Conduct user interviews. The objective of this task is to gather information that will enable both data processing and user management to evaluate the costs and benefits of the proposed project. The task steps are

- Identify operations managers and supervisory personnel to be interviewed.
- Prepare interview questionnaires.
- Schedule and conduct feasibility study interviews.
- Document feasibility study interview responses.
- Collect supporting documentation.

Task 3: Review present system.   The objective of this task is to gain an understanding of what the present system does and how it does it. The task steps are

- Review organizational functions and their relationships.
- Review the types and volumes of inputs and outputs.
- Analyze control procedures.
- Review the technical environment (i.e., hardware platforms, network facilities, and potentially reusable objects).
- Analyze control procedures (i.e., network access, database access, backup and recovery, and program control procedures).
- Identify components which may be reused in the proposed system.

Task 4: Define objectives of proposed system.   The objective of this task is to summarize the preliminary requirements of the proposed system. The task steps are

- Identify functional objectives.
- Identify regulatory and/or compliance objectives.
- Identify architectural objectives.

Task 5: Identify alternatives.   The objective of this task is to identify alternative solutions that may satisfy the user requirements.

- Identify alternatives for satisfying the functional objectives.
- Identify alternatives for satisfying the regulatory and/or compliance objectives.
- Identify alternatives for satisfying the architectural objectives.

Task 6: Evaluate costs and benefits.   The objective of this task is to compare costs to benefits to determine the economic feasibility of each development alternative. The task steps are

- Evaluate benefits to be derived from the proposed system.
- Review current operating costs and development costs.
- Compare development and operating costs to identified benefits.

Task 7: Prepare feasibility study report. The objective of this task is to prepare a report to communicate to management the results of the feasibility study. The contents of the document should summarize the analyses of

- The present system.
- The proposed system objectives.
- The development alternatives.
- The economic evaluation.

Task 8: Deliver feasibility study supporting documentation to repository. The objective of this task is to deliver the data collected during the feasibility study to the repository for indexing and maintenance.

Requirements definition

The objective of the requirements definition phase is to define the functional and physical requirements of the proposed system. The requirements definition phase breaks down into 10 major tasks.

Task 1: Review feasibility study data. The objective of this task is to review the feasibility study data maintained in the repository. The task steps are

- Review feasibility study interview summaries.
- Review supporting documents and other exhibits collected during the feasibility study.

Task 2: Conduct requirements definition interviews. The objective of this task is to gather data that expands on the data collected during the feasibility study. The task steps are

- Schedule requirements definition interviews.
- Conduct requirements definition interviews.
- Document requirements definition interview responses.
- Collect supporting documentation.
- Review requirements definition interview summaries with respondent to ensure accuracy and correct representation.

Task 3: Define object-oriented system requirements. The objective of this task is to define the functions to be performed by the system. The task steps are

- Identify actors (users).
- Identify problem domain objects.
- Write use cases to emulate specific operations.
- Define interface requirements.

Task 4: Define objects. The objective of this task is to identify each object specified in the use cases. The task steps are

- Identify objects and classes.
- Analyze object attributes.
- Describe object relationships.
- Prepare data dictionary.

Task 5: Define client and server requirements. The objective of this task is to define the requirements for establishing the client/server environment which will support the functional and architectural requirements of the system. The task steps are

- Define client hardware requirements.
- Define client software requirements.
- Define server hardware requirements.
- Define server software requirements.
- Define server data management requirements.

Task 6: Define information network service requirements. The objective of this task is to define the service-level requirements for the information network. The task steps are

- Define response time requirements.
- Define the throughput requirements.
- Define reliability and availability requirements.

Task 7: Define implementation requirements. The objective of this task is to define the physical requirements that must be satisfied in the implementation of the proposed system. The task steps are

- Define the performance requirements of the proposed system (e.g., accuracy and validity requirements, timing requirements, failure contingency requirements, and interface requirements).

- Define the environment requirements of the proposed system (e.g., equipment requirements, support software requirements, interface requirements, security and privacy requirements, control requirements).

- Define the organizational requirements of the proposed system (e.g., position changes, training requirements, job classification changes).

- Define development requirements of the proposed system (e.g., CASE tools, training requirements, time requirements).

Task 8: Identify alternatives.   The objective of this task is to identify each practical alternative to designing the system. The tasks involved are

- Identify potential software packages, networks, and/or computer hardware that may satisfy the requirements.

- Conduct research and contact vendors for additional information.

- Analyze the potential of each alternative.

Task 9: Establish criteria for evaluating alternatives.   The objective of this task is to establish the criteria for evaluating and selecting packages to be leased or purchased from computer hardware vendors and third-party software companies.

Task 10: Construct requirements model.   The objective of this task is to construct a model that extrapolates requirements from the results of tasks performed during the requirements definition. The model should consider the requirements for both object-oriented and client/server computing.

Task 11: Deliver requirements definition documentation to repository. The objective of this task is to deliver the data resulting from the task performed during the requirements definition to the repository for indexing and maintenance.

Design

The design function is accomplished in two phases: external design and internal design. The process is illustrated in Fig. 3.3.

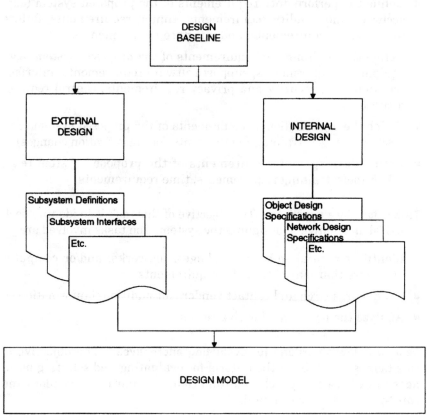

Figure 3.3   The design process

External design

The *external design* phase provides the transition from the requirements model to a set of user-oriented design models. The tasks performed are aimed at enabling the user organizations to monitor the
internal design and subsequent implementation of the system to
ensure that the requirements have been met. The external design
breaks down into 10 major tasks.

Task 1: Review requirements definition data.   The objective of this task
is to review the requirements definition data maintained in the repository. The task steps are

- Review requirements definition interview summaries.

- Review supporting documents and other exhibits collected during the requirements definition.

Task 2: Define subsystems. The objective of this task is to design the subsystems and assign tasks and objects to each subsystem. The task steps are

- Define the interface object functions.
- Define the entity object functions.
- Define the control object functions.
- Define the functional subsystems.

Task 3: Define client/server functions and allocate tasks to processors. The objective of this task is to define the functions of the client/server environment and to allocate tasks to processors. The task steps are

- Determine the mode of processing (i.e., host-based processing, client-based processing, or cooperative processing).
- Allocate the functions to be performed by clients.
- Allocate the functions to be performed by servers.

Task 4: Define subsystem interfaces. The objective of this task is to define the common boundary between independent systems or modules where communications will take place. The task steps are

- Define the hardware interfaces.
- Define the software interfaces.

Task 5: Define system security controls. The objective of this task is to define the systems controls. The task steps are

- Define physical security methods.
- Define procedural control methods.
- Define technical control methods.

Task 6: Define design constraints. The objective of this task is to define the various physical, organizational, and operational constraints which may affect the design of the system. The task steps are

- Define constraints imposed by the operating time window.
- Define constraints imposed by hardware limitations.

- Define constraints imposed by the communication environment.

Task 7: Iterate requirements and design modeling. The objective of this task is to iterate each element of the requirements and design process to ensure that the understanding acquired during the analysis and design processes is incorporated into the system model. The task steps are

- Iterate object model.
- Iterate subsystem specification.
- Iterate interface specification.

Task 8: Evaluate design alternatives. The objective of this task is to evaluate the design alternatives. The task steps are

- Evaluate alternatives for satisfying the performance requirements.
- Evaluate alternatives for satisfying the data requirements.
- Evaluate alternatives for satisfying the environmental requirements.
- Evaluate alternatives for satisfying the organizational requirements.

Task 9: Finalize preliminary design model. The final external design task is the construction of a preliminary design model. The model considers the requirements for both object-oriented and client/server computing. The object-oriented aspects of the model show the distribution of the behavior specified in the use case descriptions among the objects and how the objects are grouped to form subsystems. The client/server aspects of the model show how subsystem tasks are allocated to clients and servers. The object-oriented and client/server segmented models are then combined to create an integrated *preliminary design model* for the object-oriented client/server system to be implemented. The outputs of this task are high-level descriptions of all the subsystems and schematics of each subsystem showing the allocation of object-oriented and client/server functions.

Task 10: Deliver external design documentation to repository. The objective of this task is to deliver the data resulting from the task performed during the external design to the repository for indexing and maintenance.

Internal design

The *internal design* establishes the framework for system implementation and test. During this phase, documents are produced that specify precisely how the functional elements defined during the external design will be transformed into a physical architecture for an object-oriented client/server system. All the specifications necessary to code the application programs are included in the deliverable items. The internal design breaks down into 10 major tasks.

Task 1: Review external design data.   The objective of this task is to review the external design data maintained in the repository. The task steps are

- Review external design model.
- Review supporting documents and other exhibits collected during the external design phase.

Task 2: Design the system architecture.   The objective of this task is to design the technical elements that must be integrated in the design of the system. The task steps are

- Design the object-oriented system architecture.
- Design the client/server architecture.
- Design the resource-sharing architecture.
- Define the relational database architecture.
- Design the distributed processing architecture.

Task 3: Finalize object design.   The objective of this task is to finalize the object design in light of the actual implementation environment. The task steps are

- Define class structures in the implementation environment.
- Specify algorithms for class operations.
- Optimize object specifications for improved performance.
- Iterate class specifications for inheritance.
- Specify procedure for implementing relationships.
- Prepare specifications for instantiation.

Task 4: Specify data structures.   The objective of this task is to finalize the data specifications for providing input and output to the system. The task steps are

- Specify transaction layouts.
- Specify display layouts.

- Specify report layouts.
- Prepare output index.

Task 5: Design the databases. The objective of this task is to design the databases required to implement the system design. The task steps are

- Transform simple objects into a database design.
- Transform composite objects into a database design.
- Transform compound objects into a database design.
- Transform associations into a database design.
- Transform hybrid objects into a database design.

Task 6: Specify special design considerations. The objective of this task is to define the special considerations pertinent to the design of the system. The task steps are

- Prepare special design specifications for teleprocessing.
- Prepare special design specifications for data control.
- Prepare special design specifications for audit, security, backup, and recovery.
- Prepare design specifications for history and/or purging.
- Specify enhancement considerations.

Task 7: Finalize manual control procedures. The objective of this task is to finalize the system control procedures. The task steps are

- Finalize I/O control procedures.
- Finalize user control procedures.
- Finalize access control procedures.
- Finalize file maintenance procedures.
- Finalize recovery control procedures.
- Finalize test control procedures.
- Prepare procedure manuals.

Task 8: Define implementation and test plans. The objective of this task is to develop work plans for the implementation and testing of the system. The task steps are

- Define plans for extracting reusable object components.
- Define plans for creating new object components.
- Develop the plan for implementing the client/server system.
- Define the plan for installing the database management system (DBMS).
- Define the work plan for creating databases.
- Develop the plan for installing the application.
- Develop work plans for testing the network, application, and DBMS.

Task 9: Construct detailed design model. The objective of this task is the construction of a detailed design model. The model considers the requirements for both object-oriented and client/server computing. The object-oriented segment of the detailed design model should specify the procedures for implementing objects and subsystems. The client/server segment of the detailed design model should specify the procedures for allocating subsystem tasks to clients and servers. The object-oriented and client/server segments are then combined to create an integrated *detailed design model,* which establishes the framework for implementation and testing.

Task 10: Deliver internal design documentation to repository. The objective of this task is deliver the data resulting from the task performed during the internal design to the repository for indexing and maintenance.

Implementation and Test

The internal design established the framework for system implementation and test. During this phase, the elements specified in the design model are transformed into a physical architecture for an object-oriented client/server system. The implementation and test process breaks down into 10 major tasks.

Task 1: Review internal design data. The objective of this task is to review the design specifications maintained in the repository. The task steps are

- Review internal design model.
- Review supporting documents and other exhibits collected during the internal design phase.

Task 2: Extract reusable object components. The objective of this task is to reduce implementation costs by utilizing reusable written code. The task steps are

- Extract reusable components from C++ libraries.
- Extract reusable components from ObjectPAL libraries.
- Extract reusable components from the present system.
- Generalize extracted components.
- Customize generalized components.

Task 3: Create new components. The objective of this task is to create the software components specified in the design that are not available from or derivable from objects in the reuse libraries. The task steps are

- Create interface objects.
- Create entity objects.
- Create control objects.
- Create new methods for ObjectPAL design objects.

Task 4: Conduct unit and integration testing. The objective of this task is to conduct unit testing to ensure that the individual operations and methods behave as expected and conform to design specifications, and to conduct the integration testing for cooperating objects. The task steps are

- Update the unit test plan.
- Update the integration test plan.
- Create test specifications.
- Conduct testing.
- Correct errors and iterate.

Task 5: Prepare control program (main program). The objective of this task is to prepare the control program to ensure proper event handling, error trapping, and so on.

Task 6: Prepare user manual. The objective of this task is to prepare a user manual. The contents of the manual are divided as follows:

- General information (i.e., information that explains the purpose of the user guide and the terms and references that are subject to interpretation by the user).

- System summary (which explains the system operation, system configuration, and system performance capabilities).

- Query and update procedures (which include scenarios and step-by-step instructions for querying the databases).

Task 7: Prepare technical documentation. The objective of this task is to collect and organize the documentation needed for the operations staff and for the ongoing support of the system. The task steps are

- Prepare operations documentation that provides the operations staff with the required information to support the application.

- Prepare systems documentation that provides the ongoing support staff with the information necessary to maintain and/or enhance the application.

Task 8: Install the client/server system. The objective of this task is to implement the client/server system design. The task steps are

- Purchase network components.
- Prepare for installation.
- Install network server, cables, and software.
- Install and test network operating software, utility software, and user directories.
- Convert single-user systems to multiuser systems.
- Train users.

Task 9: Install DBMS. The objective of this task is to install the DBMS selected to facilitate the creation and maintenance of the databases. The task steps are

- Install DBMS engine.
- Install definition tools subsystem.
- Install processing interface subsystem.
- Install applications development tool subsystem.
- Install data dictionary subsystems.
- Install data administration subsystems.

Task 10: Create databases. The objective of this task is to implement the database design. The task steps are

- Define database structure to DBMS.
- Allocate media space.
- Create the database data.

Task 11: Install application. The objective of this task is to install the object-oriented application in the client/server environment. The task steps are

- Create disks.
- Load files on server.
- Load files on clients.

Task 12: Perform acceptance testing. The objective of this task is to verify and validate that the applications meet the system requirements.

Object-Oriented Client/Server Development Methodology

Part 2 of this book provides a step-by-step methodology for the development of an object-oriented client/server application. It is presented as a series of tasks and task steps. The presentation should not be taken, however, as a straight-line development. Systems development is a blend of science and art. The science is in the tools and techniques used to resolve a business or technical problem. The art is in the analysis, design, and implementation of the system. The art of development is iterative in nature. A design concept is presented, tried, and modified to improve on one or more aspects. This iterative approach is not easily represented in a book which is linear in nature. Keep in mind as you work with the methodology that you may need to reiterate through various phases. Also keep in mind that two phases may be concurrent—design may begin on a part of the system for which the analysis is completed, while the analysis continues in another area. This has potential dangers in that the further analysis may impact the area thought to have been completed, but can also expedite the development of the system.

Chapter 4, Analysis Methodology, *presents an integrated analysis methodology for the development of an object-oriented client/server application.*

In Chap. 5, Design Methodology, *the analysis results are transformed first into a preliminary design and then into an implementation model. This establishes the framework for the client / server installation and application coding.*

Chapter 6, Implementation and Test Methodology, *presents a methodological approach to the construction, test, and implementation of an object-oriented client / server system.*

4

Analysis Methodology

The analysis process is triggered by a request for a new system or system enhancement. The initiator prepares a *project request* document, which provides information about problems encountered with the present system or opportunities identified for new functionality in a new or modified system. If the request is approved by the manager of the user organization for which the system will be developed, it is forwarded to the information systems group for analysis. The methodological framework for conducting the analyses encompasses three phases: initial investigation, feasibility study, and requirements definition.

An *initial investigation* is conducted to clarify what is being requested, verify that the request cannot be adequately satisfied with existing systems (e.g., a current application already provides the requested functionality), and establish the need for the new system. If authority is granted to proceed to the next phase, the analyst conducts a feasibility study to assess the business and technical impacts of the proposed system. The tasks performed focus on reviewing the present system, defining the functional objectives of the proposed system, identifying alternative solutions, and evaluating costs and benefits. The results of the feasibility study are communicated to management for review and decision whether to proceed to the requirements definition phase.

During the requirements definition phase, the analyst expands on the functional objectives and identifies the various objects in the domain of the proposed system. The tasks performed focus on identifying and clarifying functional requirements, defining domain objects, specifying implementation requirements, identifying alternatives, and establishing criteria for alternative evaluations. The requirements definition phase culminates in the construction of a requirements model that depicts the requirements for both object-oriented and client/server computing.

Procedures for initiating an object-oriented client/server systems development project and the task orientation of each analysis activity are detailed in this chapter.

Project Request

It is the responsibility of top management to establish the procedures for initiating a project request. The procedural approach outlined below is proposed as a methodology for preparing and processing a project request for a new system or system enhancement.

Organizational flow

Regardless of the organizational form, channels for initiating and processing a project request must be developed to ensure that everyone concerned with the proposed system has a clear understanding of the responsibilities of the initiating division management, the initiator, the approving manager, the management information system (MIS) librarian, and the development group.

Initiating division management.   It is the responsibility of initiating division management to

- Identify which activities and individuals are authorized to request systems services.
- Define management review procedures to ensure that project requests are reasonable, valid, and appropriate to the situation.
- Identify the managers authorized to approve project requests and provide a list of these authorized managers to the information system (IS) management.
- Identify distribution requirements for project request replies.

Initiator.   It is the responsibility of the initiator to

- Prepare project requests which clearly and concisely describe the problem, opportunity, or suggestion and provide the background and justification necessary for analysts to evaluate the necessity or advisability of taking action.
- Coordinate the problem or suggestion with related functions to ensure that the project requests are valid and acceptable to others in the organization.

- Specifically identify the action requested and propose a solution if one has been determined.

- Obtain the approval signature of an authorized manager within the organization.

Approving manager. It is the responsibility of the group manager authorized to approve project requests to

- Assure that the subjects of project requests are appropriate to the business goals of the organization and/or enterprise.

- Assure that the requests have been coordinated with related activities and do not conflict with the requirements of other functions.

- Assure that the project requests are clear and complete.

- Approve all satisfactory project requests.

Development organization librarian. It is the responsibility of the development organization librarian to

- Assure that all project requests have been approved by an authorized manager.

- Log project requests in and out of the MIS.

- Refer project requests to the appropriate MIS entities.

- Establish a repository for maintaining project documentation and other project data.

- Prepare periodic reports of project request actions, commitments, and status as directed.

Development group. It is the responsibility of the development group to

- Investigate all project requests related to the analysis and design of the proposed system.

- Maintain ongoing communications with the initiating managers to ensure responsiveness to the user's needs.

- Identify and communicate with vendors and other external organizations that provide products and services needed to facilitate the development process.

- Assign responsibility for the analysis, design, and implementation.

- Accomplish the action committed on the project request on or prior to the estimated completion date.

Procedural flow

The steps involved in preparing and processing a project request are as follows.

Step 1: Initiation. On identification of a problem or suggestion which requires MIS action, the initiator prepares a formal project request. The initiator then reviews the request with others who may be affected by the proposed project. When the necessary coordination has been accomplished, the initiator retains a copy and forwards the project request to the approving manager for review and approval.

Step 2: Business assessment. On receipt of a project request, the approving manager conducts an investigation to assess whether the timing of the proposed project is compatible with data processing and enterprise business goals. (*Note:* The business justification of applications, equipment facilities, and other changes is outside the scope of this investigation. These areas of business concern will be the focus of the initial investigation and feasibility study phases of the systems development life cycle.)

Step 3: Approval and reply. After the preliminary investigation is completed, the approving manager will either sign the project request indicating approval or send a memo or letter to the initiator explaining why a decision was made to disapprove, delay, or cancel the project. If the project request is approved, it is forwarded to MIS.

Initial Investigation

The project request is reviewed by the MIS manager to determine how the objectives stated by the request can best be met. If the request calls for a major development effort, an analyst is assigned to conduct an initial investigation to acquire a better understanding of the problems, opportunities, and needs expressed in the project request.

Data is collected during the initial investigation that will enable the analyst to assess the problem and need as well as the anticipated benefits of implementing the proposed system. Working with the user management and key user personnel, the analyst performs a series of tasks and task steps aimed at evaluating the cost and benefits of the proposed project. The initial investigation culminates with the development of a feasibility study plan and the preparation of an initial investigation report that will lead to management approval to proceed with the project, to delay the project, or to disapprove the request.

The tasks and task steps to be performed during the initial investigation are listed in Table 4.1 and discussed in detail in subsequent paragraphs.

TABLE 4.1 Initial Investigation

Task	Task steps
1. Assess project request	Assess user needs Assess conflicts Assess compatibility with enterprise goals
2. Establish repository	Define acquisition functions Define cataloging functions Define organization functions Define circulation functions Define disposition functions Define change management procedures
3. Prepare to conduct initial investigation	Prepare work schedules Prepare for interviews Identify existing documentation
4. Conduct user interviews	Conduct initial investigation interviews Document interview responses Collect supporting documentation
5. Analyze collected documents	Analyze needs data Analyze problem data Analyze benefits data
6. Prepare feasibility study work plan	Develop plan for reviewing the present system Develop work plan for analyzing the proposed system Develop work plan for identifying development alternatives Develop work plan for identifying technical support needs Develop work plan for economic evaluation
7. Prepare initial investigation report	
8. Deliver initial investigation supporting documents to repository	

Task 1. Assess project request

The first task in the initial investigation is to assess the project request to assess the user needs, identify possible conflicts, and validate that the requested project is compatible to the enterprise goals. The methodology for assessing the project request is summarized as follows.

Assess user needs.   To assist in the evaluation of the project request, a rationale is needed for deciding which needs can be met and which needs cannot be met. The three dimensions for analyzing user needs are performance, time, and cost. The criteria for evaluating performance needs should consider all those technical and nontechnical attributes in order to determine what the requested system or system modification should do when it is completed and in operation. The criteria for evaluating timing needs pertain to all aspects of the design, such as

When is it needed?

What is the earliest time that the system can be ready?

The criteria for evaluating cost needs takes into consideration the IS and user resources required and available, and the costs of labor and overhead for the development effort.

Deliverable(s):

- Needs assessment

Assess conflicts.   The analyst should investigate the various conflicts that can greatly influence the success or failure of the development effort. The most common types of conflict in a software development environment involve schedules, priorities, workforce, technical issues, redundant functionality with existing systems, administration, personnel, and cost. Each conflict can impact the life cycle of a project. If project managers are aware of the conflicts that may occur during the various life-cycle phases, there is a likelihood that the detrimental aspects of the conflicts can be avoided or minimized.

Deliverable(s):

- List of conflicts
- Analysis of impacts

Assess compatibility with enterprise goals. Although each division or department within an enterprise may be granted authority to approve a request for system services, the request must fall within the scope of the enterprise goals. Project requests that satisfy the policy conditions will be accepted, while those that violate a policy condition may be rejected.

Deliverable(s):

- Project business compatibility assessment

Task 2. Establish repository

The *repository* combines the functions of a technical reference library, a systems documentation library, and a program maintenance library. The items contained in the repository include deliverables, phase end-documents, vendor documents, and a variety of working papers pertinent to the development of the project. The application of the project file methodology involves defining technical functions and implementing change management procedures. The methodology for establishing and managing the repository is summarized as follows.

Define acquisition functions. The *acquisition function* determines the volume and character of information maintained in the repository. It has two subfunctions: the acquisition of internally generated documents and the acquisition of externally generated documents. Various types of internally generated documents are needed to maintain an accurate historical record of a development project. These include planning, analysis, design, and implementation and testing documents. Several forms and indexes may be used to control the acquisition of documents from external sources (e.g., document requisition forms, document order records, purchase order forms).

Deliverable(s):

- Procedures for acquiring internally generated documents
- Procedures for acquiring externally generated documents

Define cataloging functions. The *cataloging function* provides a means for both identifying and locating documents in the repository. The process consists of descriptive cataloging, classification, and the preparation of indexes. When the cataloger receives a copy of the document order record, a cataloging worksheet is prepared to facilitate the cataloging function. A unique call number is assigned to each document. Separate classification schemes should be devised to differentiate between those documents generated internally and the documents acquired from outside sources. Indexing applications include conventional alphabetic indexes that provide an overview of the entire repository, category indexes that list all documents by title, and special indexes that cover a variety of user needs.

Deliverable(s):

- Procedures for cataloging, classifying, and indexing documents to be entered into the repository

Define organization functions.   The organization of the repository requires a variety of devices and filing methods. These devices and methods must accommodate all types of information media: books, correspondence, disk packs, manuals, CD-ROMs, microforms, printouts, and tape reels.

Deliverable(s):

- Plan for the physical filing and maintenance of various document formats (books and manuals, correspondence, tapes, disks, data cartridges, CDs, and printouts).

Define circulation functions.   The circulation methodology is viewed in terms of four information files that enable control of all check-in and check-out functions: (1) an authorized patron file that provides information about each individual or organization authorized to access the repository, (2) a title file that identifies each item delivered to the repository, (3) an in-circulation file that records current transactions, and (4) a hold file that contains outstanding requests for a particular configuration item currently checked out by another repository user.

Deliverable(s):

- An authorized patrons file
- A titles file

- An in-circulation file
- A hold file

Define disposition functions.   During the development cycle, the repository is generally maintained by the development organization. Once the project is completed, however, the project files may be transferred to the customers who supplied the data. Other documentation developed by the IS organization may be retained for maintenance purposes, yet other documentation may be sent to an archive location.

Deliverable(s):

- Procedures for project file disposition

Define change management procedures.   Changes in system design must be reflected in all applicable baseline documentation. Formal channels of communications must, therefore, be established between the change control authorities and the repository librarian.

Deliverable(s):

- Baseline definitions
- Baseline document revision control procedures
- Vendor document update procedures

Task 3. Prepare to conduct initial investigation

The objective of this task is to develop a work plan for conducting the initial investigation. This involves preparing documents that establish schedules for conducting interviews, identifying organizational units to be interviewed, formulating questions to be asked, and indexing existing documentation from which data can be gleaned. The methodology for preparing for the initial investigation is summarized as follows.

Prepare work schedules.   This task step involves determining the start and completion dates for each task to be performed and preparing a Gantt chart showing the start and completion dates.

Deliverable(s):

■ Initial investigation work schedule

Prepare for interviews. This task step involves identifying the organizational units to be included in the initial investigation, preparing questionnaires, and scheduling interviews.

Deliverable(s):

■ Interview schedule
■ Interview questionnaires

Identify existing documentation. This task step involves identifying both internally and externally produced documentation that presently exists from which data can be gleaned.

Deliverable(s):

■ List of existing documents

Task 4. Conduct top-management user interviews

The objective of this task is to gather, through interviews, sufficient business and technical data to apply value judgments to the problems and needs identified in the project request. Interviewees are generally selected from the ranks of top management, specifically the top-level managers of the department or function requesting the project and top managers of other enterprise organizations likely to be impacted by the proposed project. The methodology for conducting management interviews is summarized as follows.

Conduct top-management interviews. Rapport with the respondent must be established quickly. The respondent should be allowed to answer questions on an individual or personal basis, but the course of the interview must be directed by the interviewer. The interviewer must make sure that answers are in a consistent form and that all relevant topics are covered in the brief time available for the interview. The initial investigation interviews general focus on functions currently performed; clarification of the problems identified in the project request; a brief analysis of the potential improvements specified in the project request; and the identification of organizational units, budgets, and personnel affected by the proposed project.

Deliverable(s):

- Interview worksheets

Document top-management interview responses. Interview summaries should be prepared in a standard format. The response summary should provide for referencing the questions asked, identifying the respondent, summarizing the response, prioritizing the need (e.g., mandatory, highly desirable, desirable), categorizing the problem (e.g., turnaround time, volume processing, network access), and assessing the benefit (e.g., operating costs, quality of service, timeliness of information, operating productivity). The initial investigation interviews are then reviewed with the respondent to ensure accuracy and correct representation.

Deliverable(s):

- Interview summaries

Collect supporting documents. The supporting documents collected may include organization charts, key input and output documents, reports that address the topics under investigation, advisory letters from auditors, and recommendations from outside consultants.

Deliverable(s):

- Supporting documents

Task 5. Analyze collected data

Analysis of the interview summaries and supporting documents involves tabulating the interview responses and assessing the current needs, problems, opportunities, and benefits of the proposed system. The methodology for analyzing the collected data is summarized as follows.

Analyze needs data. This task step addresses the level of need. Because needs expressed in the project request may not be accurately or completely represented, a matrix analysis process can be used to assess the need. Three principal levels may be predefined in the needs assessment: mandatory, highly desirable, and desirable.

Deliverable(s):

■ Needs assessment

Analyze problem data. This task step focuses on assessing the problem indicated in the project request. The analyst conducting the initial investigation analyzes the problem data with respect to the user's understanding of the system and the information collected. The problem areas may be categorized as technical or informational. The analyst may, of course, add other categories as deemed appropriate.

Deliverable(s):

■ Problem definition statement

Analyze benefits data. This task step focuses on assessing the benefits to be derived from the proposed system. In assessing the benefits of the proposed project, the analyst views the system from several perspectives: operating costs, quality of service, timeliness of information, operating productivity, and efficiency of service.

Deliverable(s):

■ Benefits analysis

Task 6. Prepare feasibility study work plan

The purpose of this task is to prepare a plan for conducting a feasibility study. The plan defines procedures for reviewing the present system, determining preliminary requirements of the proposed system, identifying package alternatives, and analyzing costs and benefits. The methodology for preparing a feasibility study work plan is summarized as follows.

Develop plan for reviewing the present system. The plan for reviewing the present system focuses on identifying existing documentation, defining present system functions, identifying inputs and outputs, reviewing current costs, and amplifying the problem and need analyses of the initial investigation.

Deliverable(s):

- Present system review work plan

Develop work plan for analyzing the proposed system. The plan for analyzing the proposed system focuses on identifying the minimum objectives, identifying the output requirements, defining a conceptual approach, identifying input requirements, and analyzing organizational and environmental implications.

Deliverable(s):

- Proposed system analysis work plan

Develop work plan for identifying development alternatives. The plan for identifying development alternatives outlines a methodological approach for reviewing alternative approaches to development, identifying available packages and vendors, and establishing criteria for evaluating development alternatives.

Deliverable(s):

- Work plan for alternatives analysis

Develop work plan for identifying technical support needs. The plan for identifying technical support needs outlines a methodological approach for the tasks to be performed during the feasibility study to define the data management approach, analyze communications needs, and evaluate hardware and software characteristics.

Deliverable(s):

- Technical support need identification work plan

Develop work plan for economic evaluation.   The plan for economic evaluation outlines procedures for reviewing current operating costs and benefits, projecting the costs and benefits of the proposed system, and analyzing intangible costs and benefits.

Deliverable(s):

■ Economic evaluation work plan

Task 7. Prepare initial investigation report

The objective of this task is to present the findings of the initial investigation to management. The task is accomplished by synthesizing and reorganizing the items that document the results of the tasks performed during the initial investigation.

Deliverable(s):

■ Initial investigation report

Task 8. Deliver initial investigation supporting documentation to repository

The objective of this task is to transfer all documentation and exhibits resulting from the initial investigation to the project repository for cataloging and maintenance.

Feasibility Study

The *feasibility study* is concerned with providing management with sufficient data to permit intelligent decision making regarding the economic justification and technical feasibility of the proposed project. The tasks performed during the feasibility study phase focus on defining the characteristics of the existing system and analyzing the objectives of the proposed system. The tasks and task steps to be performed during the feasibility study are listed in Table 4.2 and discussed in detail in subsequent paragraphs.

Task 1. Review initial investigation data

The first task in the feasibility study is to review the documentation delivered to the repository at the conclusion of the initial investiga-

TABLE 4.2   Feasibility Study

Task	Task steps
1. Review initial investigation data	
2. Conduct feasibility study interviews	Identify the operations managers and supervisory personnel to be interviewed Prepare interview questionnaires Schedule and conduct feasibility study interviews Prepare feasibility study interview summaries Collect supporting documentation
3. Review present system	Review organizational functions and their relationships Review the types and volumes of inputs and outputs Analyze control procedures Review the technical environment Identify reusable components
4. Define objectives of proposed system	Identify functional objectives Identify regulatory and/or compliance objectives Identify architectural objectives
5. Identify alternatives	Identify alternatives for satisfying the functional objectives Identify alternatives for satisfying regulatory and/or compliance objectives Identify alternatives for satisfying architectural objectives
6. Evaluate costs and benefits	Evaluate benefits Evaluate costs Assess value of the proposed project
7. Prepare feasibility study report	
8. Deliver feasibility study documentation to repository	

tion to ensure an understanding of management objectives in relation to the project.

Task 2. Conduct feasibility study interviews

During the initial investigation, top managers who control the organizational resources were interviewed. In the conduct of feasibility study interviews, the emphasis is on assessing the feasibility of the proposed project from the perspective of operations managers and supervisory personnel. The methodology for conducting these user interviews is summarized as follows.

Identify the operations managers and supervisory personnel to be interviewed. The objective of this task is to identify the operations managers and supervisory personnel to be interviewed for details about user functions, problems, and needs. A job profile should be prepared for each prospective interviewee. The format for preparing the job profile should consider the following: (1) identification of the person to be interviewed; (2) identification of the division, department, and/or section or group; (3) a general description of the technical and administrative duties performed; (4) interfaces with other departments; and (5) qualifications of the interviewee (i.e., why this person was selected for the interview).

Deliverable(s):

■ Job profile of each person to be interviewed

Prepare interview questionnaires. The objective of this task is to prepare the questions to be asked in gathering information about user problems and requirements. The list of questions should be coordinated with all project team members who will conduct the interviews.

Deliverable(s):

■ List of questions to be asked during the interviews

Schedule and conduct feasibility study interviews. The objective of this task is to schedule and conduct the interviews with operations managers and supervisory personnel. The focus of the interviews should be on gathering information about the present methods, procedures, systems, work processes, operations, and so on, and the identification of the proposed system objectives.

Deliverable(s):

■ Interview schedules
■ Interview worksheets for documenting the responses during the interview

---

Prepare feasibility study interview summaries. The objective of this task is to prepare interview responses and review the contents with the respondent to ensure accuracy and correct representation.

Deliverable(s):

- Summaries of the respondent's answers to the questions asked

Collect supporting documentation. As in the case of the initial investigation, the supporting documentation collected may include organization charts, key input and output documents, reports that address the topics under investigation, advisory letters from auditors, and recommendations from outside consultants.

Deliverable(s):

- Collected documents, charts, reports, and other materials that provide data pertinent to the feasibility assessment

Task 3. Review present system

The objective of this task is to gain an understanding of what the present system does and how it does it. The review processes focus on analyzing the organizational functions and their relationships, the types and volumes of inputs and outputs, the technical environment (hardware, platforms, network facilities, etc.), control procedures, and components which may be reused in the proposed system. The methodology for reviewing the present system is summarized as follows.

Review organizational functions and their relationships. The objective of this task step is to analyze the organizational structure. Data is gathered that will help the analyst understand how authority is granted to individuals who make decisions for others to follow, how responsibilities are delegated to individuals, and which organizational elements are accountable for the satisfactory completion of a specific assignment.

Deliverable(s):

- Charts that schematically portray the user organization for whom the proposed system will be developed

- A user organization profile form that provides details about each user organization included in the analysis

---

Review the types and volumes of inputs and outputs. This task step focuses on identifying the information requirements of the system and analyzing the input/output requirements, including the volume, distribution, and frequency of inputs and outputs.

Deliverable(s):

- An input summary form that identifies each document, transaction, and file that provides input to the present system
- An output or report summary that identifies each report or other output media generated by the present system

---

Analyze control procedures. This task step focuses on analyzing the security and privacy requirements and the control considerations or constraints imposed on the user.

Deliverable(s):

- A security, privacy, and controls summary for the current system

---

Review the technical environment. The objective of this task is to review the existing environment to identify the strengths and weaknesses of the existing technical environment. The task includes analysis of the existing hardware platforms and their configurations, network facilities, software libraries, and applications.

Deliverable(s):

- Configuration identification of existing hardware and software environment, with descriptions of the strengths and weaknesses of each component

---

Identify reusable components. The objective of this task is to identify whether any parts of the existing system are reusable within the new system. Emphasis is on identifying reusable object components, reusable interface objects, and reusable control objects. In identifying the reusable components, note whether the component can be used as is or will require modification.

Deliverable(s):

- List of present system components which may be reused in the development and implementation of the proposed system

---

Task 4. Define objectives of proposed system

The objective of this task is to summarize the preliminary requirements of the proposed system. The task steps focus on identifying the object-oriented, client/server, and networking objectives of the proposed system. The methodology for defining the objectives of the proposed system is summarized as follows.

Identify functional objectives. This task step focuses on identifying the functions to be supported by the proposed application. The analysis should describe the function, identify its relative importance, and indicate the reason for the function.

Deliverable(s):

- A list of proposed system functions, ranked by relative importance

---

Identify regulatory and/or compliance objectives. This task step focuses on identifying the objectives of the system in relation to any regulatory or compliance requirements such as regulatory compliance reports or fulfillment of audit discrepancies.

Deliverable(s):

- A list of regulatory and compliance objectives to be satisfied by the proposed system

---

Identify architectural objectives. This task step focuses on identifying the objectives of the proposed system in terms of technology or data architecture requirements. Emphasis is on identifying the object-oriented, client/server, and network architecture issues addressed by the development of the new application.

Deliverable(s):

- A list of information technology architectural objectives, classified as to whether the objective to be satisfied by the system is an applications architecture, data architecture, network architecture, or other objective

Task 5. Identify alternatives

The objective of this task is to identify the alternatives for satisfying the requirements of the proposed system. The methodology for identifying alternatives is summarized as follows.

Identify alternatives for satisfying the functional objectives.   This task step focuses on identifying package alternatives to satisfy the functional objectives of the proposed system.

Deliverable(s):

- A list of commercially available or other available application packages which may satisfy some or all of the functional objectives of the proposed system

Identify alternatives for satisfying regulatory/compliance objectives.   This task step focuses on identifying available alternatives for satisfying the regulatory and/or compliance objectives of the proposed system.

Deliverable(s):

- A list of commercially available or other available application packages which may satisfy some or all of the regulatory and/or compliance objectives of the proposed system

Identify alternatives for satisfying architectural objectives.   This task step focuses on identifying alternatives for accomplishing the architectural objectives of the proposed system.

Deliverable(s):

- A list of software packages [e.g., applications development toolkits, programming utilities, compilers and languages, computer-aided software engineering (CASE) tools, systems development techniques] that may satisfy the architectural objectives of the proposed system

- A list of hardware devices which may satisfy the architectural objectives of the proposed system

---

Task 6. Evaluate costs and benefits

The objective of this task is to evaluate the benefits and cost of developing and implementing the proposed system. The methodology for defining the objectives of the proposed system is summarized as follows.

Evaluate benefits. This task step involves identifying and evaluating benefits. While savings and avoided costs are certainly factors to be considered in justifying development of the proposed project, the focus in this task step is on evaluating benefits to achieve some specific business improvement. To quantify benefits, they must be measured against the defined objectives of the proposed system.

Deliverable(s):

- A list of tangible benefits to be derived from the proposed system
- A list of intangible benefits which are difficult to measure, but which contribute to the overall objectives of the business

---

Evaluate costs. In evaluating the costs of a proposed project, the analyst should consider all costs. Costs of both the existing and the proposed system must be evaluated. Costs may be divided into two general categories: development costs and ongoing recurring costs. Development costs include the costs of personnel, equipment, materials and supplies, conversion of records and procedures, structuring the database, hardware and software packages, and training. Recurring costs must include the ongoing costs of operating the system, including operations, data preparation, control, and maintenance.

Deliverable(s):

- A *current operating costs* form that tabulates costs associated with the present system
- A *proposed system operating costs* form that tabulates the projected ongoing costs of the proposed system

- A *development cost estimating* form that presents the phase-by-phase estimates of the cost to develop the system

---

Assess value of the proposed project. Having evaluated the benefits and costs, the analyst focuses on assessing the value of the proposed project to the enterprise. If a charge-back procedure is used, the responsibility of the development organization is to make a reliable estimate of the cost of the system to be built. If the enterprise does not have a charge-back procedure, then the analyst must explicitly relate costs and benefits and provide sufficient information for management assessment of the value of the project.

Deliverable(s):

- A *cost comparison* form that summarizes and compares the operating cost data of the present and proposed systems
- A *return-on-investment* form that calculates the savings that may be generated through the proposed system and estimates the return on investment over the expected life of the system

---

Task 7. Prepare feasibility study report

The objective of this task is to present the findings of the feasibility study to management. The task is accomplished by synthesizing and reorganizing the items that document the results of the tasks performed during the feasibility study.

Deliverable(s):

- A report that reflects the analyses conducted during the feasibility study, culminating in a recommendation of whether to continue with the system development effort

---

Task 8. Deliver feasibility study documentation to repository

The objective of this task is to transfer all documentation and exhibits resulting from the feasibility study to the project repository for cataloging and maintenance.

Requirements Definition

The objective of the requirements definition is to define the functional and physical requirements of the proposed system. Object-oriented functional requirements are defined in terms of users, interface requirements, problem domain objects, and extraction of data types. Client and server functions are defined in terms of messaging, communications, and shared resource requirements. The tasks and task steps to be performed during the requirements definition phase are listed in Table 4.3 and discussed in detail in subsequent paragraphs.

Task 1. Review feasibility study data

The first task in the requirements definition is to review the documentation delivered to the repository at the conclusion of the feasibility study. These documents are reviewed to ensure that the objectives identified during the feasibility study are incorporated in the development of the requirements definition activities.

Task 2. Conduct requirements definition interviews

The interview methodology developed and implemented during the initial investigation and feasibility study phases is iterated in the requirements definition phase. The methodology for conducting the requirements definition interviews is summarized as follows.

Identify personnel to be interviewed.   The objective of this task is to identify the top managers, operating managers, and supervisory personnel to be interviewed to amplify the data collected during the initial investigation and feasibility study phases.

Deliverable(s):

- Job profiles of each person to be interviewed

Prepare interview questionnaires.   The objective of this task is to prepare the questions to be asked in gathering information about user problems and requirements. The list of questions should be coordinated with all project team members who will conduct the interviews.

TABLE 4.3   Requirements Definition

Task	Task steps
1. Review feasibility study data	
2. Conduct requirements definition interviews	Identify personnel to be interviewed Prepare interview questionnaires Schedule and conduct requirements definition interviews Prepare requirements definition interview summaries Collect supporting documentation
3. Define object-oriented system requirements	Identify actors (users) Identify problem domains Write use cases to emulate specific operations Define interface requirements
4. Define objects	Identify objects and classes Analyze object attributes Describe object relationships Prepare data dictionary
5. Define client/server requirements	Define client hardware requirements Define client software requirements Define server hardware requirements Define server software requirements Define server data management requirements
6. Define information network service requirements	Define response time requirements Define throughput requirements Define reliability and availability requirements
7. Define implementation requirements	Define performance requirements Define environment requirements Define organizational requirements Define development requirements
8. Identify alternatives	
9. Establish criteria for evaluating alternatives	
10. Construct requirements model	
11. Deliver requirements definition documentation to repository	

Deliverable(s):

■ List of questions to be asked during the interviews

Schedule and conduct requirements definition interviews.   The objective of this task is to schedule and conduct the interviews with the individuals to be interviewed. The focus of the interviews should be on defining the functional and physical requirements of the proposed system.

Deliverable(s):

- Interview schedules
- Interview worksheets that document the responses during the interview

Prepare requirements definition interview summaries. The objective of this task is to prepare interview responses and review the contents with the respondent to ensure accuracy and correct representation.

Deliverable(s):

- Summaries of the respondent's answers to the questions asked

Collect supporting documentation. As in the case of the initial investigation and feasibility studies, the support documentation collected may include organization charts, key input and output documents, reports that address the topics under investigation, advisory letters from auditors, and recommendations from outside consultants.

Deliverable(s):

- Collected documents, charts, reports, and other materials that provide data pertinent to defining the requirements of the proposed system

Task 3. Define object-oriented system requirements

The objective of this task is to define the object functions to be performed by the system. The task steps include identifying actors, writing use cases, defining interface requirements, and identifying objects and object domains. The methodology for defining object-oriented functional requirements is summarized as follows.

Identify actors (users). The objective of this task step is to identify the actors that will interact with the system. The term *actor* is used in object-oriented models to denote any object external to the system that is linked to the input and output data flow. The actor may be the user, another system, a client, or a server. For example, in an export management system, both the exporter and the importer are outside the system but are the actors who interact with the system. If the export management system derives input from an external system (e.g., the National Trade Data Bank developed by the U.S. Department of Commerce), the external system is also considered an actor. Each actor plays one or more specific roles. Actors are categorized as primary actors or secondary actors. Clients and users that interact with the system directly are called *primary actors*. Entities responsible for managing and maintaining the system (e.g., DBMSs that facilitate the creation and maintenance of a database) are called *secondary actors*.

Deliverable(s):

- List all external *actors* linked to the input or output data flow

---

Identify problem domains.   A *domain,* in the context of object-oriented client/server development methodology, is a set of objects with which an actor can interact. The problem domain consists of all elements with which the system must concern itself in fulfilling its function. By specifying the domain in this manner, the use cases prepared in the next step can be more completely specified. Also, the specification of the problem domain allows us to determine those elements which are not part of the system under development.

Deliverable(s):

- A *problem domain analysis* that identifies and describes the entities that constitute the proposed system

---

Write use cases to emulate specific operations.   *Use cases* define the specific operations to be performed by the system in response to events initiated by actors. A use case is written for each sequence of related transactions performed in a dialog between the actor and the system. By writing use cases for each actor, the analyst, in effect, defines the complete functionality of the system being developed.

Deliverable(s):

- Use cases for each of the functions the system will perform

Define interface requirements. Interface descriptions are an essential part of a use case description. The interface must reflect the user's logical view of the system. Thus, prior to designing interfaces, the user's interaction with the system must be clearly defined and a description of the interaction should be included in the use case written for each user (actor). In addition, other system interfaces (e.g., communications protocols) should be defined during this task step.

Deliverable(s):

- An *interface analysis* document that describes the media, frequency, and purpose of each interface between organizations, functions, and operations

Task 4. Define objects

The objective of this task is to define the objects specified by the use cases and problem domains. The task steps include identifying objects, creating an object dictionary, identifying associations and attributes, organizing object classes using inheritance, and verifying access paths. The methodology for defining system objects is summarized as follows.

Identify objects and classes. An *object* can be thought of as an entity that encapsulates both the data and the operations that generate the actions of the object. These object operations are sometimes called *methods*. Objects are identified by first analyzing the use cases to determine the operations to be performed by the application. Objects that require the same set of resources for their execution are grouped to form an object class. The process of defining classes, assigning operations to the classes, and grouping classes will be iterated during the requirements definition, external design, and internal design. Each iteration will provide a level of detail, but also incorporate improved understanding resulting from additional experience with the system objects.

Deliverable(s):

- A list of objects categorized by function

Analyze object attributes. Objects represent specific instances of a class. The *instance* is defined by a unique combination of attributes associated with the class. Attributes may identify an object or be intrinsic to the class—making the object an instance of a specific class. Each object must have at least one identifier, but may have multiple identifiers. Attributes that are intrinsic to each instance of the object are termed *descriptive attributes*. Attributes used to name or label instances are termed *naming attributes*. Attributes used to link an instance of one object to an instance of another object are termed *link attributes*. Define the attributes of each object and the range of values that each attribute can assume.

Deliverable(s):

- List of attributes for each object
- Definition of range of values for each attribute

Describe object relationships. A *relationship* is defined as any dependence between two or more object classes. The relationships may be classified as either *unconditional relationships* or *conditional relationships*. In the unconditional relationship, every instance of an object is required to participate in the relationship. In a conditional relationship, some instances of the object may not be required to participate in the relationship. If the relationship between both objects is conditional, the relationship is termed *biconditional*. Relationships can also be described in terms of their cardinality (one-to-one, one-to-many, many-to-many, etc.) This step of object definition focuses on defining relationships in terms of the states of instances (attribute values) of one object in relation to the states of other object instances. The objective of this task step is to prepare a written description of each relationship. The descriptions should include the identifier of the relationship, a statement of the basis of abstraction, an expression of the form of the relationship, and a statement of how the relationship is formalized.

Deliverable(s):

- An *object relationship diagram* showing the relationships between objects and the cardinality of the relationships
- A state diagram showing the variations in attribute value based on changes in another object.

Prepare data dictionary. The objective of this task is to create a centralized repository of information about each object or object class in an application domain. The object descriptions should concentrate on describing the attributes, operations, and roles of each object or class of objects. The descriptions are a vital part of the database management system that provides information on the nature and usage of the stored objects.

Deliverable(s):

- A *project data dictionary* with definitions of each object class, with attributes and relationships specified.

Task 5. Define client/server requirements

The objective of this task is to define the requirements that are prerequisite to client/server computing. The task steps include defining client hardware and software requirements, server software and hardware requirements, and server data management requirements. The methodology for defining the client/server functional requirements is summarized as follows.

Define client hardware requirements. The objectives of this task step is to define the front-end hardware requirements for processing client-based, host-based, and cooperative processing applications. The requirements definition should consider the memory required to load and execute application logic, and the amount of data to be stored locally.

Deliverable(s):

- A *client hardware requirements* document that identifies the workstation, adapter card, and cabling requirements of the client environment

---

Define client software requirements. The objective of this task is to define the client software requirements. The client software requirements to be considered include the network interface software requirements, the application programs supporting the user requirements, and utilities which utilize the network capabilities (e-mail, groupware, etc.). The network interface software should provide the functions prescribed by the OSI model.

Deliverable(s):

■ A *client software requirements* document that identifies the operating system, applications, and utilities software requirements of the client environment

Define server hardware requirements. The objective of this task is to define the server hardware requirements. The types of servers considered in the requirements definition are file servers, application servers, data servers, compute servers, database servers, and communications servers.

Deliverable(s):

■ A *server hardware requirements* specification that identifies the computers, adapters, and cabling requirements for the server environment

Define server software requirements. The objective of this task is to define the server software requirements for managing the network, providing access to data residing on the server storage devices, generating data requests for data residing on other nodes, and transmitting requests to the appropriate server.

Deliverable(s):

■ A *server software requirements* specification that identifies the operating systems, applications, and utilities software requirements for the server environment

Define server data management requirements. The objective of this task is to define server data management requirements. The analysis process focuses on defining the SQL linkage requirements, access requirements, distributed database requirements, protocols for remote data access, data management software requirements, and database gateway requirements.

Deliverable(s):

■ A *server data management requirements* specification that identifies the SQL linkage, database access, and distributed processing requirements of the proposed system

---

Task 6. Define information network service requirements

The objective of this task is to define service-level requirements of the information network that are likely to influence the design of the network architecture and topology. The task steps include defining the response time requirements, throughput requirements, and reliability requirements. The methodology for defining the information network service requirements is summarized as follows.

Define the response time requirements. The response time requirements should be measured in terms of the defined object-oriented client/server functional requirements. For on-line and interactive workloads, the response time should be measured as the elapsed time from the moment the client is ready to transmit to the time the entire response is received from the server. The response time measurement thus considers all activities required in satisfying the request, including field editing, message routing, message interpretation, and message calculation.

Deliverable(s):

- Documentation that defines the time constraints that must be placed on the proposed system relative to attaining a specified output after an input is received

---

Define the throughput requirements. Throughput should be measured in terms of the amount of useful work that must be performed by the system in a given period of time. The analysis of throughput requirements focuses on the speed of the communication links, the speed of the switching nodes, the amount of memory required for storing messages in transit, and the software overhead imposed by the protocol stack.

Deliverable(s):

- Documentation that defines the amount of useful work that the proposed system must be able to perform in a given period of time

Define reliability and availability requirements. The analysis of *reliability requirements* focuses on the ability of the system to perform its function under specified conditions for a stated period of time. The overall reliability is measured in terms of the mean time between failures, the mean time to repair, and the mean time to recover. The analysis of *availability requirement* is defined as the extent to which the system is operable when required.

Deliverable(s):

- Documentation that specifies the reliability requirement in terms of the mean time between failures, the time to repair, and the mean time to recover

- A statement specifying the percentage of time the system must be operational

---

Task 7. Define implementation requirements

The objective of this task is to define the physical requirements that must be satisfied in the implementation of the proposed system. The task steps include defining the performance, environmental organizational, and development requirements. The methodology for defining implementation requirements is summarized as follows.

Define performance requirements. The objective of this task is to define the specific performance requirements to be satisfied by the new system. The requirements should be stated in such a manner that they can be linked back to the system functions defined during the feasibility study and that the system test activities can be tied back to them. A quantitative presentation of the requirements should be included (e.g., number of records that must be handled, maximum allowed time from query to receipt of requested information, and flexibility required to accommodate changing user requirements. Specific areas for which requirements must be defined include requirements pertaining to the accuracy and validity of mathematical calculations and data and failure contingency requirements (e.g., backup, fallback, and restart).

Deliverable(s):

- A matrix of system functions and performance measurements that the system must achieve in accomplishing each function

---

Define environment requirements. The objective of this task is to define the environmental requirements for satisfying the performance requirements. Specific areas of analysis concern include the hardware platform, operating system, DBMS, and network environments in which the computer programs must operate. Also included in the analysis are the requirements for interfacing with other systems; security and privacy requirements, and control requirements.

Deliverable(s):

■ Documentation that identifies the environmental framework in which the system must operate

Define organizational requirements. The objective of this task to define the organizational impacts of the proposed system, including the modification of positional responsibilities and the addition or elimination of responsibilities that will be necessary to implement the new system.

Deliverable(s):

■ Documentation that defines the organizational impacts of implementing the new system

Define development requirements. The objective of this task is to define the development requirements (e.g., CASE tools, training, staffing, and the amount of the user's time that will be required to facilitate the systems development process). This task also encompasses requirements for temporary help, special consultant services, and other services which are needed during the development but not as part of the ongoing operation of the system.

Deliverable(s):

■ Documentation that defines the development requirements of the new system

Task 8. Identify alternatives

The objective of this task is to identify each practical alternative to designing the system. A narrative description of each alternative should be prepared that defines the expected implementation approach and explains how it differs from other alternatives.

Deliverable(s):

- List of potentially viable alternatives
- A brief description of each alternative describing which functions will be addressed by the alternative

Task 9. Establish criteria for evaluating alternatives

The objective of this task is to establish the criteria for evaluating and selecting from among the various alternatives. This will include evaluation criteria for hardware and software packages to be leased or purchased from external vendors.

Deliverable(s):

- A set of criteria by which the various alternatives can be evaluated

Task 10. Construct requirements model

The objective of this task is to construct a model that extrapolates requirements from the results of tasks performed during the requirements definition. The model should consider the requirements for object-oriented computing, client/server computing, and network performance. The object-oriented segment of the model should address the static structure of objects (object modeling), the sequencing of interactions (dynamic modeling), and object transformations (functional modeling). The client/server aspects should address the requirements for resource sharing, distributed processing, and relational database processing. The network performance segment of the model should address network connectivity and network management issues.

Deliverable(s):

- An expansion of the object model created in task 4, incorporating the constraints imposed by the various requirements identified in subsequent tasks

- A client/server network requirements model identifying the functional and operational requirements of the client, server, and network components

---

Task 11. Deliver requirements definition documentation to repository

The objective of this task is to transfer all documentation and exhibits resulting from the requirements definition to the project repository for cataloging and maintenance.

5

Design Methodology

During the system design phase, the requirements reflected in the requirements model are translated into a set of specifications that can be used during the implementation and test phase. The process is concerned with the respecification of the system objectives to define the design constraints, determining the mode of system operation, establishing the operation capability, selecting the physical equipment needed, and specifying the functional structure of the system and the system components. The methodological framework for designing the system breaks the work to be performed into two phases: external design and internal design. The external design specifies the system in non-implementation-specific terms, whereas the internal design incorporates the hardware, DBMS, and programming language-specific specifications.

The overall design approach consists of continual refinement and iteration to ensure completeness and robustness. The objects identified in the analysis process represented real-world objects. During the design, additional objects will be added to control and monitor event and operation logic. As design progresses, the objects will be grouped and the interfaces between the groups (subsystems) will be defined. In the next step, the intrasubsystem (i.e., object-to-object) behaviors are defined. This refinement of granularity continues, until at the end of the internal design, each object is specified in terms of its data, attributes, operations, and instantiation.

External Design

The *external design* phase provides the transition from the requirements model to a set of user-oriented design models. During the external design phase, the subsystems are defined and functions allocated to each subsystem, client/server functions are defined and functions are allocated to processors, the basic structure and access to application data stores are specified, system and user interfaces are identified, the DBMS is selected, the procedural requirements for communication and system control are formalized, and the appropriate package alternatives for satisfying the system requirements are selected. The tasks and task steps to be performed during the external design are listed in Table 5.1 and discussed in detail in subsequent paragraphs. It should be remembered that object-oriented development is an iterative process which results from improved understanding as analysis and design proceed. We should also remember that the sequence of tasks may be altered or that parallel

TABLE 5.1   External Design

Task	Task steps
1. Review requirements definition data	
2. Define subsystems	Define interface object functions Define entity object functions Define control object functions Define the functional subsystems
3. Define client and server functions and allocate tasks to clients and servers	Determine the mode of processing Allocate functions to be performed by clients Allocate functions to be performed by servers
4. Define subsystem interfaces	Define hardware interfaces Define software interfaces
5. Define system security controls	Define physical control methods Define procedural control methods Define technical control methods
6. Define design constraints	Define constraints imposed on the system by the operating-time window Define constraints imposed on the system by the hardware Define constraints imposed on the system by the communication environment
7. Iterate requirements and design modeling	Iterate object model Iterate subsystem specification Iterate interface specification
8. Evaluate design alternatives	
9. Finalize preliminary design model	
10. Deliver external design documentation to repository	

activities may take place to contribute to the complete understanding of the system design needs.

Task 1. Review requirements definition data

The first task in the external design is to review the documentation delivered to the repository at the conclusion of the requirements definition. You will use the object and class definitions and other aspects of the requirements definition model during the external design. The review should focus on the identification of requirements which may affect the choice of processors or subsystem allocations for the various functions and objects identified in the requirements definition.

Task 2. Define subsystems

The objective of this task is to design the subsystems and assign tasks and objects to each subsystem. The design activities focus on defining entity, interface, and control object functions; grouping objects by attributes to form applications modules; and decomposing the system into subsystems. Objects identified in the requirements definition with common attributes are likely candidates for grouping into subsystems. The methodology for defining subsystems and allocating functions is summarized as follows.

Define interface object functions. *Interface objects* represent functionality (specified in the use case descriptions) that is dependent on the interface to the system and subsystems. There are two types of interface objects: (1) objects that are interfaces to human users and (2) objects that are interfaces to other systems. User interface objects translate the user actions into events that provide for bidirectional communications between the user and the system. In this task step, the functions of the interface objects identified in the object model created during the requirements definition are more precisely defined. Additional interface objects may be specified, or functions may be split among objects to assist in distinguishing classes.

Deliverable(s):

- An updated object model with interface functions more precisely defined
- An updated data dictionary with interface object functionality specified

---

Define entity objects functions. An *entity object* is an object or event about which information is stored beyond the life of the object. (This is known as *persistent data* because it persists beyond the time the object exists.) Information about the object's attributes is stored in the database (e.g., a record in a marketing database that contains name, address, and telephone number of a prospective customer). This task step defines the functions performed by the entity objects.

Several different strategies may be used to allocate functionality specified in the use case. For example, computation or embedded control can be allocated to entity objects and control objects, reducing the functionality of the interface objects; or dialog dominant control of inquiries and related responses in an interactive session may be allocated to the interface objects, thus reducing the functionality of the control objects. The type of control allocated to the interface objects will depend, to a great extent, on the application being designed.

Deliverable(s):

- An updated object model with entity object functions more precisely defined
- An updated data dictionary with entity object functionality specified

Define control object functions. *Control objects* are objects which do not fit either of the first two categories. They typically involve more than one of the other objects and act to coordinate information between objects or perform calculations using information from multiple objects. Because control object functionality extends across more than one object, specification of their functionality will typically be more complex than that of either interface or entity objects.

Deliverable(s):

- An updated object model with control object functions more precisely defined
- An updated data dictionary with control object functionality specified

Define the functional subsystems. The objective of this task is to decompose the system into subsystems. The task involves grouping object classes into logically distinct modules. The object classes should be grouped to create logical subsets of the subsystem model. For example, a subsystem may contain modules for process control, device control, file maintenance, and memory management. A common starting point for this process is to analyze the attributes of the various objects. Those objects sharing similar attributes are likely candidates for grouping into a subsystem.

Deliverable(s):

- A system model depicting the modular grouping of objects (and functionality) into application subsystems.

Task 3. Define client/server functions and allocate tasks to clients and servers

The objective of this task is to define the client/server functions and to allocate each concurrent subsystem task to the clients and servers. In assigning subsystem tasks to processors, the designer must take into consideration the tasks required to control hardware or permit independent or concurrent operation, the available communication bandwidth between a task and a piece of hardware, and the need to spread tasks between processors when the computation rates are too great for a single processor. The methodology for defining client/server functions and allocating tasks to processors is summarized as follows.

Determine the mode of processing.   The processing of a given function in a client/server application can be accomplished in any one of three processing modes: (1) host-based processing, (2) client-based processing, or (3) cooperative processing. Each mode of processing places a different demand on the client, the server, and the network. In a host-processing mode, the presentation logic, application logic, and DBMS run on the server/host. The server/host interacts with the client software which provides for graphical front-end displays. In a client-based processing mode, the function logic runs on the client processor and data queries are sent to the server, which provides the answer back to the client for continued processing or presentation. The data validation routines are coded into the DBMS on the server. In a cooperative processing mode, a peer-to-peer processing approach is used. The application logic resides on both the client and the server and the data can be manipulated by both. The presentation logic runs on the client.

Deliverable(s):

- A *processing specification* document that defines the mode of processing for each operation performed by the system, along with specification of the formula, calculations, and algorithms to accomplish the operation

Allocate the functions to be performed by clients. The objective of this task is to allocate to clients those functions required to issue requests for server processing, perform the various user interface functions, compose messages to be sent to servers, send messages to servers, receive messages from servers, and decompose the messages received. If different functionality is required at different clients, distinguish the client category when allocating functionality.

Deliverable(s):

- A *client function allocation* worksheet that identifies the objects that will reside on the client to provide the required functionality and achieve the required performance

Allocate the functions to be performed by servers. The objective of this task is to allocate to servers those functions required to receive messages from clients, control multiple client requests, decompose messages from clients, execute program code, compose messages to be sent to clients, and send messages to clients.

Deliverable(s):

- A *server allocation* worksheet that specifies those objects that will reside on the server

Task 4. Define subsystem interfaces

The objective of this task is to define the events initiated by one subsystem, but which require action by one or more other subsystems. The methodology for defining subsystem interfaces is summarized as follows.

Define hardware interfaces. Specify communications content to and from hardware devices such as scanners, printers, bar-code readers, keypads, and mice. Each of these devices should be defined as interface objects in task 2.

Deliverable(s):

- A *hardware interface* specification that identifies the data content and format for cross-platform and device communications

---

Define software interfaces.   Specify the communications content between subsystems. Identify the events that precipitate the communication and the actions triggered by the communication in the receiving subsystem.

Deliverable(s):

- A *software interface* specification that identifies the data content of communications between software systems and subsystems
- A matrix showing the events and the software interface communications triggered by each event

---

Task 5. Define system security controls

The objective of this task is to define the physical, procedural, and technical methods for controlling system security. The methodology for defining system controls is summarized as follows.

Define physical control methods.   Physical control methods must be devised to restrict access to the system. Passwords and access codes are examples of physical controls. Other methods of physical security include using lock and key techniques. For example, the keyboard may be locked when not in use. Likewise, floppy disks or other removable media can be maintained under lock.

Deliverable(s):

- A *control specifications* document that specifies the procedures for controlling the physical environment

---

Define procedural control methods.   *Procedural controls* govern use of the computer. One approach to procedural control is to make users totally accountable for their data, equipment, and passwords. This accountability can be an important part of training users. To help maintain the integrity of the data a control procedure can be defined that requires that users make their intentions known before they can access data. Another way is make sure that each user makes backup copies of the work performed and maintains proper logs and documents.

Deliverable(s):

- A *control specifications* document that specifies the user procedures for ensuring integrity of the data

Define technical control methods. *Technical controls* built into the system can screen out unauthorized users and restrict what authorized users are allowed to do. The built-in controls can be configured to automatically shut down the system after more than two or three attempts to enter an improper password. The built-in controls can also impose identification and access procedures for the use and transfer of data and establish audit trails. Another built-in method for backing up personal computer data should also be considered. Software-based control functions in an object-oriented environment may introduce new objects (both control objects and interface objects), or add functionality to previously identified objects. Update the object models and the data dictionary with any new objects or functions.

Deliverable(s):

- A *technical control specifications* document that defines the software-based control procedures built into the system
- Updated object model, dynamic model, and function models
- Updated data dictionary

Task 6. Define design constraints

The objective of this task is to define the various constraints which may impact the internal design process. Constraints identified here will drive decisions which could lead to design changes or determinations to modify the constraining conditions. The methodology for preparing special design specifications is summarized as follows.

Define constraints imposed on the system by the operating-time window.
If there are operating-time window constraints imposed by business
requirements, network maintenance activities, or other factors which
reduce the system availability to other than a 24-h-per-day, 7-day-
per-week basis, then those constraints must be identified in the external design. These may impact the implementation design where
assumptions might otherwise be made about long-running transactions or retention of data in active memory rather than writing to the
database.

Deliverable(s):

- An *operating–time window constraints specification* that describes
  constraints on the operational availability of the system

Define constraints imposed on the system by the hardware.   If there are
known hardware constraints which might impact further development decisions, those constraints must be specified. Such constraints
might, for instance, describe hardware interfaces with nonstandard
word sizes, or speed limitations which could impact performance.

Deliverable(s):

- A *hardware constraints specification* that identified any constraints imposed on the design of the system by hardware interfaces, operating platforms, or peripheral devices with which the
  system must communicate

**Define constraints imposed on the system by the communication environ-
ment.**   Known constraints imposed by the communications environment which might impact design decisions must be identified. For
example, a designer of a system to be accessed from remote locations
would need to be aware of the least common communications speeds
available to the remote sites to ensure proper functionality (perhaps
necessitating a buffering mechanism).

Deliverable(s):

- A *communications constraint specification* that identifies the constraints imposed by the communications environment

**Task 7. Iterate requirements and
design modeling**

The objective of this task is to iterate each element of the requirements definition model, taking into consideration the increased
understanding of the requirements derived from the tasks performed
during the external design. The task steps are as follows.

Iterate object model. Add or relocate objects, operations, or associations based on information gained through the development of subsystems. Review the use cases to ensure that all dynamic information
is captured in the model. Clarify object definitions with descriptions
of attribute ranges and events triggering changes to the attributes.

Deliverable(s):

- Updated object model
- Updated data dictionary, reflecting changes to the object model

Iterate Subsystem Specification. Review the subsystem definitions to
ensure that all functions specified in the requirements are allocated
and that any new functions identified in the external design process
are included. If required, adjust the subsystems to reflect the new
information. It may be appropriate to iterate more than once, depending on the number of changes and the degree of complexity.

Deliverable(s):

- Updated subsystem specification

Iterate interface specifications. Review the specification for interface
communications and update the specification to reflect changes in the
object model and the subsystem allocation of function. New information gathered during the external design may affect decisions on
which subsystem handles certain of the interface communications.
The objective is to ensure a robust system at the time of implementation, which can be modified when required without requiring changes
to every object or every subsystem.

Deliverable(s):

- Updated interface specification

Task 8. Evaluate design alternatives

The various hardware, software, and DBMS alternatives identified in the requirements definition are evaluated against the design criteria developed in the external design. Each of the various alternatives evaluated must be analyzed in terms of cost, applicability for use beyond the current development effort, and value to the project.

Deliverable(s):

- An *alternatives evaluation matrix* that tabulates and compares the features of the candidate products
- A narrative description of the chosen alternatives explaining the reasons for selection

Task 9. Finalize preliminary design model

The objective of this task is to construct a preliminary design model that depicts the subsystems and the functions allocated to each subsystem, the client/server functions and how they are allocated to processors, the basic database structure and how data is accessed, the system and user interfaces, the DBMS used to facilitate the creation and maintenance of the databases, and the procedural requirements for communication and system control. The model should be reviewed with the users to ensure completeness and agreement in terms of the functions residing on various platforms. Various reports from the data dictionary may be appropriate in communicating the functions associated with the objects and subsystems.

Deliverable(s):

- A preliminary design model
- Data dictionary reports

Task 10. Deliver external design documentation to repository

The objective of this task is to deliver the data resulting from the tasks performed during the external design to the repository for indexing and maintenance.

Internal Design

The *internal design* establishes the framework for system implementation and test. During the internal design phase, the processing architecture for the object-oriented client/server system is formalized, and object designs are finalized, reflecting the actual implementation environment; specifications are prepared for transaction processing, table, file, and report and display design; control procedures for ensuring database and file integrity, facilitating error correction and system auditing, and controlling database and file access are formalized; and procedures for implementation and testing are established. The tasks and task steps to be performed during the internal design are listed in Table 5.2 and discussed in detail in subsequent paragraphs.

Task 1. Review external design data

The first task in the internal design is to review the documentation delivered to the repository at the conclusion of the external design. Specific focus is placed on the preliminary design model to ensure understanding of the system domain and the nature of the environment.

Task 2. Design the system architecture

The objective of this task is to design each technical element required for system implementation and to integrate these elements to establish the overall system architecture. The strategies for designing each technical element take into consideration design factors relative to the network, hardware, operating system, databases, software, and utilities required for effective operation. The methodology for designing the integrated system architecture is summarized as follows.

Design the object-oriented system architecture.   The object-oriented architectural segment of the integrated system includes the selection of the programming language and potentially the selection of an object-oriented database system. The selection of the programming language can be viewed from an object-oriented or an object-based perspective. When using an object-oriented programming language, programmers can create their own object types. C++ is an object-oriented language. When using an object-based programming language, new object types cannot be created. ObjectPAL is an object-based programming language. ObjectPAL limits the creation of objects to only those that can be derived from the object types that are predefined by

TABLE 5.2   Internal Design

Task	Task steps
1. Review external design data	
2. Design the system architecture	Design the object-oriented system architecture Design the client/server architecture Design the resource-sharing architecture Define the database architecture Design the distributed processing architecture
3. Finalize object design	Define class structure in implementation environment Specify algorithms for class operations Optimize the object specifications for improved improvements Iterate class specifications for inheritance Prepare specifications for implementing relationships Prepare specifications for instantiation
4. Specify data structures	Specify transaction layouts Specify display layouts Specify report layouts Prepare output index
5. Design the databases	Transform simple objects into a database design Transform composite objects into a database design Transform compound objects into a database design Transform association objects into a database design Transform hybrid objects into a database design
6. Specify special design considerations	Specify teleprocessing considerations Specify special data control considerations Specify special security considerations Specify history and purging considerations Specify enhancement considerations
7. Finalize manual control procedures	Finalize I/O control procedures Finalize user control procedures Finalize access control procedures Finalize file maintenance procedures Finalize recovery control procedures Finalize test control procedures Prepare procedure manuals
8. Define implementation and test plans	Define plans for extracting reusable object components Develop work plan for creating new object components Develop plan for implementing the client/server system Define plans for installing the DBMS Define plan for creating databases Develop plan for installing applications Define plans for testing applications
9. Construct detailed design model	
10. Deliver design documentation to repository	

the language itself. The choice of language is dependent on the needs of the organization. The features of C++ provide greater flexibility in development, but the integrated Paradox for Windows environment provides a much easier development environment. It is often advantageous to use ObjectPAL for front-end (client systems) development and use C++ for the back-end and control object definitions. ObjectPAL is integrated with the Paradox for Windows database environment. For client/server computing, Borland offers the SQL Link product, which enables the ObjectPAL programs to communicate with several relational database systems on the server platform via embedded SQL statements. Numerous other languages and development environments can, of course, be selected depending on the needs and available skill sets of the development organization. Many of the object-oriented DBMSs have an integrated language.

Deliverable(s):

- *Object-oriented language specification*

Design the client/server architecture.   The client/server architectural segment of the integrated system defines the configuration of computers to be connected in a network. The clients manage the user interface, accept data from the user, process application logic, generate database requests and receive server responses, and format the response to generate reports and screen displays. The servers accept database requests from clients, process the database requests, transmit the response to clients, perform integrity checking, maintain database overhead data, provide concurrent access control, perform recovery tasks, and optimize query and update processing.

Networks can be configured in many ways. In a *bus network,* a single communication circuit is shared by every node, but the circuit is not joined together to form a loop. In a *ring network,* all the nodes are connected together in a ring, with none having overall control of access to the network. In a *star network,* a device or hub acts as the clearinghouse through which all messages pass. The network designer may want to consider several variations of these networks. These include a *loop network,* in which all the nodes are connected together in a ring, but one of them controls the rest; a *tree network,* in which the nodes are connected by a branching communication channel; a *mesh network,* in which the nodes are interconnected in a unique manner which cannot be classified in terms of the other topologies; and a *fully interconnected network,* in which each node is directly connected to every other node in the network by a link that is not shared with any other.

Connectivity is a vital area of concern in the client/server architecture. Design decisions must be made regarding the physical media that will enable the clients and servers to exchange communications (e.g., coaxial cables, optical fiber connections, connectors, repeaters, terminators, wireless network media), the network standards that will be used (Ethernet, IEEE 802.3, etc.), communications protocols [Xerox Network System (XNS) Layered Architecture, Internetwork Datagram Protocol, Routing Information Protocol, Sequenced Packet Protocol, Packet Exchange Protocol, etc.], and network synchronous communications services (e.g., parallel communications and serial communications). The network operating system is the heart of the client/server network. Choosing the right network operating system is a vital part of the design effort. Novell, Microsoft, and 3Com are primary vendors of client/server network operating systems. IBM, Digital Equipment Corp. (DEC), and other hardware vendors also provide network operating software.

In addition, the system designers must take into consideration the network management approach related to configuring, monitoring, controlling, and analyzing the resources on the network; optimizing the use of those resources; and preventing and solving user problems.

Deliverable(s):

- A *network design specification* that defines the number and location(s) of servers and of client platforms, identifies the transmission media (coaxial, twisted-pair, fiber-optic, etc.) and the physical path of the media; specifies the network interface to the clients and servers; and specifies the routers, hubs, gateways, repeaters, and other devices required to fully configure the network

---

Design the resource-sharing architecture. The *resource-sharing* architectural segment of the integrated system translates the processor allocations performed in the external design to physical specification of devices on which the function will reside. This allocation should map to the network design specification created in the last step. Allocation of resources is a function of the capabilities of the hardware, operating systems, and application components. Resource-sharing networks are frequently used for applications that require fast disks for storage of large single-user files, large spreadsheets, and so on. Printers, plotters, and other peripheral equipment are commonly shared. As functions are allocated to the various client and server platforms, the designer should review the hardware specifications to ensure that the platform can operate within the performance specifications developed during the requirements definition and external design processes.

Deliverable(s):

- A *resource allocation matrix* that identifies the objects, databases, operating system, and other system resources that will reside on each client and server in the network

---

Define the database architecture.   The database management system selected for the application may be defined by the object-oriented architecture specified earlier in this task. If not, however, it must be done at this time. Selection of the database architecture will be based on the nature of the application. Transaction-based systems in which the focus of the application is the capture of data and the manipulation of records will be best suited for a relational database system. Applications focusing on navigating and analyzing large volumes of complex data types will more likely select an object-oriented database management system. Numerous hybrid DBMSs are available which are essentially relational systems incorporating complex data types [binary large objects (BLOBs), arrays, tables, etc.].

More than one DBMS may be used in the application. For instance, a local database may reside on the client systems in a Paradox database while the primary application database resides in another relational or object-oriented database on the server.

Deliverable(s):

- A specification of the DBMS(s) for the application

Design the distributed processing architecture.   The *distributed processing* architectural segment of the integrated system provides a flexible and scalable environment for the distribution of processing functions and data to the locations where they are needed. In a distributed processing environment, both data and processes are distributed. Enterprise data can be spread over multiple systems by distributing the data and the DBMS. The *distributed database management system* (DDBMS) consists of the collection of distributed transaction and database managers on all computers. The *distributed transaction* *manager* (DTM) program receives processing requests from query or transaction programs and translates them into actions for the database manager. The *database manager program* receives and updates user and overhead data in accordance with commands received from the DTMs.

Deliverable(s):

- A specification for the distributed processing environment, expanding on the allocation of functions to platforms, and the distribution of data among the client and server platforms

---

Task 3. Finalize object design

The objective of this task is to finalize the object design in light of the actual implementation environment. The object model created during the requirements definition and expanded on during the external design did not provide any implementation specific data. At this point, however, the programming language and the DBMS come into play. The methodology for transforming the object model into an implementation-specific model is summarized as follows.

Define class structures in implementation environment. The objects in the object model have encapsulated both data and operations. In this step, we evaluate the constructs of the language and data management system to determine the best implementation approach for the classes. The implementation may specify that objects be developed as subclasses of the original class developed in the object model, and that instances be derived from one or more base classes on the basis of the state information and event generating the instance. This process may result in the addition of new classes, or the migration of functions between classes or between subclass and superclasses. For example, it might be necessary to create several versions of an operation with each version specific to each subclass.

Deliverable(s):

- Detailed class specification defining the public and private data and operations of each class and describing the differences among polymorphic operations (operations of the same name with different implementation in each subclass)

Specify algorithms for class operations. For each operation defined in the previous task step, provide detailed specifications for the implementation of each operation. This includes the specification of algorithms, formulas, and processing logic. The specification of operations may result in the definition of new control classes or subclasses within the existing class hierarchy.

Deliverable(s):

- A detailed class operation specification for each class that identifies the logic for the operation, the responsibility for the operation, and the data structure necessary to implement the operation

---

Optimize the object specifications for improved performance. As the operations are defined, the relationships among objects may be clarified, or alternate paths of accessing an object may be defined. This task step involves reviewing the current class definitions and adding operations or defining indexes on attributes which will provide improved performance in the implementation environment.

Deliverable(s):

- Updated class specification and class operation specification to reflect changes for performance improvement

---

Iterate class specifications for inheritance. Simplification of object design facilitates the reuse of the object in other applications. This simplification can be accomplished by maximizing the use of inheritance in class definitions. This step involves a further review of the class specification and module definitions to determine whether rearrangement or redefinition of classes and operations can improve inheritance. Objects with common operations may be generalized to create new base classes from which the subclasses can be derived. Do not replace roles and states with inheritance. These can better be handled using domains for the object attributes.

Deliverable(s):

- Updated class specification
- Updated class operation specification

Prepare specifications for implementing relationships. Relationships are implemented through the control objects which define the flow and access of information throughout the application. As the system design proceeds, the links between objects are updated. In this step, the events that cause objects to respond are defined and the necessary logic to implement the relationships are specified. Thus, if a one-to-many relationship exists such that a change in the one object elicits a corresponding change to each of the other objects, the logic for accomplishing that change must be assigned to a control object and the logic defined. If the focus must be returned to the initiating object, the logic must also provide the notification events needed.

Deliverable(s):

■ Detailed logic specifications for each control object to ensure that every relationship specified in the object model is implemented

Prepare specifications for instantiation. Once the operations and structure of each class in the object model are defined, it is necessary to define the mechanism by which the object instances are generated during program execution. This involves specifying the object state (values of each attribute) when initiated. In C++, this is done using object constructors and assigning values to the attributes. This task step specifies how those attributes will be assigned. They may be fixed values based on the event that causes the object to be generated, or there may be an interaction with the user of the system to establish initial values.

Deliverable(s):

■ Specifications for instantiating each object instance

Task 4. Specify data structures

The objective of this task is to specify the data structures for inputs and outputs from the system. The methodology for specifying data structures is summarized as follows.

Specify transaction layouts. The objective of this task is to specify the layouts for each transaction.

Deliverable(s):

- Specification for the data types and formats within each transaction

Specify display layouts. The objective of this task is to specify the layouts for all display screen outputs.

Deliverable(s):

- Specification for the presentation of all interface objects, defining how they will appear on the display, the location on the display, and the representation of the various attributes

Specify report layouts. The objective of this task is to specify the layouts for all report outputs.

Deliverable(s):

- Report layouts for all printed outputs for the system
- Screen layouts for all display outputs

Prepare output index. The objective of this task is to prepare a cross-reference index of all the outputs to be generated by the system. The index should identify the events and associated objects which generate the output; describe each data element on the output; and define the source and format for the data in the output record, report, or screen. This index may be generated as an output of the data dictionary if all pertinent data has been maintained in the dictionary.

Deliverable(s):

- Detailed output index

Task 5. Design the databases

The objective of this task is to design the databases that support the implementation of the applications. In a relational database model, this task involves transforming the object model into relational database designs. The design of databases underlies the architecture for an object-oriented client/server system. To represent an entity object with a relation, the designer must define a relation for the object and place the properties within its attributes. That property then becomes the key of the relationship. The use of normal forms in a database reduces problems in the manipulation and storage of data which arise from inherent interrelationships between attributes. Therefore, once a relationship has been defined for an entity, it should be examined according to normalization criteria. In transforming objects into relations, the designer must consider each type of object separately. The methodology for designing the databases is summarized as follows.

Transform simple objects into a database design. *Simple objects* contain only single-valued, nonobject properties. Each property object is defined as an attribute of the relation.

Deliverable(s):

- Initial database design

Transform composite objects into a database design. *Composite objects* contain one or more nonobject multivalued properties. In transforming composite objects that have one or more multivalued properties or groups, the designer must establish a relation for the base object and then an additional relation for the repeating composite group.

Deliverable(s):

- Composite object database design

Transform compound objects into a database design. *Compound objects* are objects that contain at least one object property. The relationships of compound objects involve some variation of one-to-one, one-to-many, or many-to-many relationships. To represent these objects in a database, the designer needs to address these three types of relations. In a one-to-one relation, we define one relation for each object, than place the key of either relation as a foreign key in the other. In a one-to-many or many-to-one relationship, each object is represented by a relation and the key of the parent (multivalued object) is set in the child. In many-to-many relationships, a relation is defined for each of the objects and third is established for the intersection relation. The intersection relation consist of the keys of both parents.

Deliverable(s):

■ Compound object database design

Transform association objects into a database design. An *association object* is an object that relates two or more objects together and stores data that is peculiar to their relationship. To represent association objects, the relationship for each object must be defined. This is a special case of the many-to-many relationship, and can be derived in the same manner.

Deliverable(s):

■ Association object database design

Transform hybrid objects into a database design. A *hybrid object* is an object that involves the combination of compound and composite objects in which the object property occurs in a composite group. To represent hybrid objects with relations, the database designer must establish one relation for the object itself, one for each object property, and another relation for each of the contained objects.

Deliverable(s):

■ Hybrid object database design

Task 6. Specify special design considerations

The objective of this task is to specify special considerations pertinent to the design of the system. The methodology for preparing special design specifications is summarized as follows.

Specify special teleprocessing considerations. The objective of this task is to specify any special considerations for interfacing the communications control software with hardware and the applications programs. This process iterates the hardware and software interface design to ensure that interface objects incorporate all requirements.

Deliverable(s):

- Updated *interface object specifications*
- Updated *class operation specifications*

Specify special data control considerations. The objective of this task is to specify any special considerations for data control and audit trail handling. This task iterates the control object design specification to incorporate additional requirements and ensure that all modifications created during the internal design have not inadvertently lost required functionality.

Deliverable(s):

- Updated *control object specifications*

Specify special security considerations. The objective of this task is to specify any special considerations for implementing the system security requirements. This task iterates the manual procedure and control object specifications to ensure that security functions are properly handled between the system and manual processes.

Deliverable(s):

- Updated *manual control procedure specifications*
- Updated *control object specifications*

Specify history and purging considerations. The objective of this task is to specify special design considerations for moving data to history or purging data from the system.

Deliverable(s):

- Updated *manual control procedure specifications*
- Updated *control object specifications*
- Updated *database design specifications*

Specify enhancement considerations. The objective of this task is to specify special considerations that must be incorporated in the design to facilitate future enhancements.

Deliverable(s):

■ Iteration of all internal design outputs to ensure maximum flexibility for enhancement

---

Task 7. Finalize manual control procedures

The objective of this task is to finalize the system control procedures. This task results in several written procedures. These are drafts which will be finalized during the implementation phase. The methodology for finalizing system control procedures is summarized as follows.

Finalize I/O control procedures. The objective of this task is to finalize the procedures used by either the clients and processors to control inputs and outputs.

Deliverable(s):

■ Manual I/O control procedure

Finalize user control procedures. The objective of this task is to finalize the user procedures required by the system in submitting and receiving information from clients.

Deliverable(s):

■ Draft user procedure

Finalize access control procedures. The objective of this task is to finalize procedures for restricting use of the applications to authorized parties.

Deliverable(s):

■ Draft access control procedure

Finalize file maintenance procedures. The objective of this task is to finalize procedures for ensuring that file maintenance transactions are properly handled.

Deliverable(s):

■ Draft file retention and backup procedure

Finalize recovery control procedures. The objective of this task is to finalize procedures for reestablishing operations after system failures and/or correction of program errors.

Deliverable(s):

■ Draft operations run procedure

Test control procedures. The objective of this task is to conduct a walk-through test of all control procedures for completeness and understandability. Update the procedures as required.

Deliverable(s):

■ Updated procedures

Prepare procedure manuals. The objective of this task is to prepare procedure manuals that can be used for user training and operations.

Deliverable(s):

■ *Draft user guide*
■ *Draft operations guide*

Task 8. Define implementation and test plans

The objective of this task is to develop work plans for the implementation and test phase. The methodology for developing the implementation and test plans is summarized as follows.

Define plans for extracting reusable object components. The objective of this task is to define the plans for extracting reusable components from C++ libraries, ObjectPAL libraries, and the present system; and defining procedures for generalizing extracted components and customizing generalized components.

Deliverable(s):

- Plan for object reuse

Develop work plan for creating new object components. The objective of this task is to develop the work plan for creating new object components from C++, including application objects, interface objects, event-handling objects, windows objects, menu objects, dialog box objects, doc/view objects, control objects, printer objects, and graphic objects.

Deliverable(s):

- Plan for new object creation

Develop plan for implementing the client/server system. The objective of this task is to develop a detailed work plan for implementing the client/server system, specifically plans for installing network servers, cables, and software; setting up and testing all network operating software, utility software, user directories, and security; converting single-user systems to multiversion systems; and training end users on how to operate the system.

Deliverable(s):

- Client/server implementation and test plan

Define plan for installing DBMS. The objective of this task is to develop the detailed work plan for installing the DBMS engine, the definition tools subsystem, the processing interface subsystem, the development tool subsystem, and the data dictionary and data administration subsystem.

Deliverable(s):

- DBMS implementation and test plan

Define work plan for creating databases. The objective of this task is to develop a work plan for defining the database structure to DBMS, allocating media space, and creating the database data.

Deliverable(s):

- Database creation work plan

Develop plan for installing applications. The objective of this task is to define the plans for installing applications, specifically plans for creating disks, loading files onto server, and loading files onto clients.

Deliverable(s):

- Application installation plan

Define plans for testing applications. The objective of this task is to define the plans for testing applications, specifically plans for conducting unit tests, integration tests, and acceptance tests.

Deliverable(s):

- Unit test plans that identify how each class and operation will be tested
- Integration test plans that identify how the related objects and subsystems will be tested for appropriate response to events
- Acceptance test plans to identify how user acceptance testing will be conducted

Task 9. Construct detailed design model

The objective of this task is to construct a detailed design model that depicts the processing architecture for the object-oriented client/server system, object design specifications, transaction processing specifications, report and display design, control plans for ensuring database and file integrity, error correction and system auditing, controlling database and file access plans, and plans for implementation and testing.

Deliverable(s):

- A detailed design model that incorporates all aspects of the internal design product

**Task 10. Deliver detailed design
documentation to repository**

The objective of this task is to deliver the data resulting from the tasks performed during the internal design to the repository for indexing and maintenance.

6

Implementation and Test Methodology

The implementation and test plans conceptualized during the analysis and finalized during the design phase are executed during this phase of the software development effort. Many of the tasks of the implementation process are performed in parallel, or in a cyclic process. For instance, the testing process is interwoven with the coding activity. Similarly, installation of the network, client, and server platforms must be accomplished in order to test the functionality of various application components. Likewise, databases must be created in the development environment before development of the entity objects can be completed. The implementation process itself is integrated throughout the development methodology. As portions of the design are completed, the objects can be extracted from existing libraries or created to meet the design criteria. The tasks and task steps to be performed during the implementation and test phase are listed in Table 6.1 and discussed in detail in subsequent paragraphs.

Task 1: Review internal design data

The first task in the implementation is to review the documentation delivered to the repository at the conclusion of the internal design. Specific emphasis is on analyzing the implementation and test plans prepared during the internal design to establish assignments and schedules for completing the tasks. The next step is to review the design model with the project team to ensure that all aspects and dependencies are well understood by all.

TABLE 6.1   Implementation of Test Tasks and Task Steps

Task	Task steps
1. Review internal design data	
2. Extract reusable object components	Extract reusable object components for C++ libraries
	Extract reusable components from ObjectPAL
	Extract reusable object components from the company reuse library
	Extract reusable object components from the existing application
	Generalize extracted components
	Customize generalized components
3. Create new object components	Create interface objects
	Create entity objects
	Create new control objects
	Create new methods for ObjectPAL design objects
4. Conduct unit and integration testing	Update unit test plan
	Update integration test plan
	Create test specifications
	Conduct testing
	Correct errors and iterate testing
5. Prepare control program (main program)	
6. Prepare user documentation	
7. Prepare technical documentation	Prepare operations guide
	Prepare systems documentation
8. Install the client/server system	Purchase network components
	Prepare for installation
	Install the network components
9. Install DBMS subsystems	Install the DBMS engine subsystem
	Install definition tools subsystem
	Install database access subsystem
	Install applications tool subsystem
	Install data dictionary and data administration subsystem
10. Implement the database	Define the database structure to the DBMS
	Allocate media space
	Create the database data
11. Install application	
12. Perform acceptance tests	

Deliverable(s):

- Updated project plan indicating the task to be performed, the person(s) assigned to perform the task, and the schedule for completion

Task 2: Extract reusable object components

The objective of this task is to reduce implementation costs and schedule by utilizing reusable resources from the code libraries and from the existing application. The task involves extracting reusable components from C++ libraries, ObjectPAL libraries, and the present system. The methodology for extracting reusable object components is summarized as follows.

Extract reusable object components from C++ libraries. C++ libraries vary from vendor to vendor. The extraction of reusable object components from a C++ library depends on the building blocks provided by the specific vendor program. The approach to extracting reusable object components outlined in this book is based on the facilities available through Borland's C++ 4.0. The types of objects that can be extracted from Borland's C++ libraries include applications objects, interface objects, event-handling objects, Window objects, menu objects, dialog box objects, `doc/view` objects, control objects, printer objects, graphic objects, and validator objects.

Deliverable(s):

- C++ object components from the vendor class libraries
- C++ object components from the company reuse library

Extract reusable object components from ObjectPAL. The extraction of reusable object components from the ObjectPAL library is dictated by the ObjectPAL language. ObjectPAL design objects have built-in code defining their default behavior. Custom code can, however, be attached to any of the design objects. This task involves extracting those custom methods appropriate to the application from a reuse library.

Deliverable(s):

- ObjectPAL reusable components from the company reuse library

Extract reusable object components from the existing application. If the new system is a replacement or enhancement to an existing system, the likelihood that many of the objects in that system can be reused is high. This task involves reviewing the existing application components and copying the reusable elements into the work environment.

Deliverable(s):

- Reusable C++ components from existing application
- Reusable ObjectPAL components from existing application

Generalize extracted components. Those components extracted from the existing application or the company reuse libraries may be too specific for use in the current project. However, with generalization of the classes or operations within the classes (methods in ObjectPAL), the objects can become generally useful in the current and future applications. These generalized classes may then be used to derive subclasses appropriate to the existing applications. These generalized objects should be forwarded to the configuration manager for inclusion within the reuse libraries.

Deliverable(s):

- Generalized C++ class structures with derived subclasses
- Generalized ObjectPAL methods for use in the application

Customize generalized components. After having created the general class structures and methods from the extracted components, the developer can now create the appropriate derived classes to meet the design specifications. *Customization* generally includes modifying the instantiation parameters to meet the specific requirements of the new system.

Deliverable(s):

- Customized C++ classes for use in the application
- Customized ObjectPAL methods, forms, and other design objects for use in the application

Task 3: Create new object components

The objective of this task is to create the software components specified in the design that are not available in the existing reuse libraries. When a new object is created, the object-oriented language used must allocate storage for its attribute values and must assign it a unique object identification number (ID). Objects in ObjectPAL, one of the object-oriented languages considered in this book, are specific to that and therefore new objects cannot be created. C++, the other programming language considered in this book, does provide for the creation of new objects. The methodology for creating new objects in C++ is summarized as follows.

Create interface objects.   Code the interface objects in compliance with the design specifications prepared during the internal design. Document the code to assist maintenance staff and developers who may reuse the objects created in understanding the purpose and behavior of the object.

Deliverable(s):

- Coded interface classes available for use in the current application and reuse from the library

---

Create entity objects.   Those objects about which information must be retained beyond the execution of the program must be created. Operations within these objects must produce output consistent with the database specifications defined in the internal design. Again, documentation of the class purpose and behavior should be included in the code and recorded in the data dictionary, if not entered during the internal design.

Deliverable(s):

- New entity objects available for use in the current application and reuse

---

Create new control objects.   The objects which control the interaction of other objects must be coded to allow full functionality of the system. These objects must be coded in compliance with the design specification and documented to support reuse and maintenance.

Deliverable(s):

- New control classes available for use in the current application and reuse

---

Create new methods for ObjectPAL design objects. The ObjectPAL components of the new system must be coded to provide the custom functionality specified in the internal design. The customized methods should be documented and made available in the reuse library.

Deliverable(s):

- Custom ObjectPAL methods available for use in the application and for reuse from the library

---

Task 4: Conduct unit and integration testing

Testing of the application components is conducted as each component is completed. The individual operations are tested to ensure that they function as expected and that the constructors and destructors behave as expected in generating and removing instances of the objects. As more components are completed, integration testing ensures that the communication among the objects generates the anticipated response. The methodology for unit and integration testing is summarized as follows.

Update unit test plan. The unit test plan was developed during the internal design process. This plan is reviewed to assign responsibilities for the testing consistent with the assignment for development.

Deliverable(s):

- Updated unit test plan

Update integration test plan. The integration test plan developed during the internal design is updated to show responsibilities consistent with the assignment of development tasks and to schedule testing to coincide with the completion of the various application objects.

Deliverable(s):

- Updated integration test plan

Create test specifications. *Test specifications* identify the test steps and the expected results from the test process. The specifications are based on the requirements and design specifications for functionality and for performance. A specification should be developed for each class and for each combination of cooperating classes created or extracted to accomplish an application objective.

Deliverable(s):

- Unit test specifications
- Integration test specifications

Conduct testing. The test process is integrated throughout the development activity. As coding is completed for one class or method, the corresponding unit test should be conducted. This ensures that any design problems are uncovered as early as possible in the development process. Tests should be conducted according to the test specifications, and discrepancies should be noted on the specification for decision on the proper resolution.

Deliverable(s):

- Tested C++ classes
- Tested ObjectPAL objects
- Documentation of discrepancies encountered in the test process

---

Correct errors and iterate testing. As discrepancies between anticipated and actual results are encountered, the discrepancy must be examined to determine whether the problem is a design problem, an implementation problem, or an incorrect test specification. When the determination is made, the correction must be made to the design, program code, or test specification. Once corrected, the testing must be repeated to ensure the proper operation of the component(s).

Deliverable(s):

- Corrected, retested application components

Task 5: Prepare control program (main program)

In a C++ program, the initial object instantiation is controlled by the main program file, which also sets up the preprocessor directives and defines the various components to be included within the application. ObjectPAL applications are controlled from a form. This task involves generating the appropriate C++ programs and ObjectPAL forms to coordinate the creation of object instances, destruction of those instances, and communications among the objects.

Deliverable(s):

- Main C++ program(s)
- ObjectPAL application forms

Task 6: Prepare user documentation

The objective of this task is to prepare user documentation that summarizes the system applications and operations functions, describes the overall performance capabilities of the system, and defines procedures that the user must follow to operate the system. Specifically, the user documentation should include step-by-step procedures for accessing the system, interacting with the system, entering required data, generating reports, and processing queries applicable to the database.

Deliverable(s):

- User guide(s) providing instruction on how to access and interface with the various system components

Task 7: Prepare technical documentation

The objective of this task is to prepare the operations documentation and the systems documentation required to operate and maintain the system.

Prepare operations guide. The operations documentation extracts the operations related specification information developed in the internal design and provides that information in a format usable to the operations staff. This information includes the backup and recovery procedures, the restart procedures, call list for program problems, and other data needed by the operations staff.

Deliverable(s):

- Operations documentation

Prepare systems documentation. This task collates the information about the purpose and design of the system relevant to the maintenance and enhancement activities. The information may be extracted from the data dictionary or collected from the project repository. The documentation should include the purpose of the application; descriptions of the programs, classes, databases, and other components of the system; and information regarding design constraints and assumptions identified in the development efforts.

Deliverable(s):

- System documentation

Task 8: Install the client/server system

The objective of this task is to install the network clients, servers, cables, and software that make up the client/server system configuration. The task involves setting up and testing all network operating software, utility software, user directors, and security. The methodology for installing the client/server system is summarized as follows.

Purchase network components. The process of acquiring the components needed to install the client/server system configuration is accomplished in several steps. The first step is to invite select vendors to submit bids. Once quotations are received from the various vendors, they should be evaluated in terms of the requirements to be satisfied. The evaluation of each quotation should take into consideration the service, warranty, price, and payment terms. When all the quotations have been evaluated, a decision is made to award a contract or issue a purchase order to the selected vendor who will provide the required components.

Deliverable(s):

- Network components including cables, connectors, network cards, workstations, servers, and network operating system

---

Prepare for installation. Prior to installation of the acquired components, various tasks must be performed. The network cabling to all the workstations should be pulled and tested. The network operating and utility software must be loaded on the server(s) and tested. The backup device on the server(s) must be tested. The hard disks on all workstations must be backed up and purged. A standard network configuration for workstations must be developed and tested. The user network menu should be developed and tested, and network administrators should be trained.

Deliverable(s):

- Validated network components
- Media installed according to network design specification

Install the network components. The first step in installing network components is to verify and label the backups of all data. The next step is to install a network card and software in one of the workstations and test the installation. If the performance is satisfactory, a network card and software is installed in the remaining workstations. Similarly, the primary network printer should be installed and tested. If the performance is adequate, the remaining printers should be installed. Other steps which may be included in the installation process include installing utility software in the appropriate devices, testing the utility software to confirm that it works, converting single-user data to a central file server, installing multiuser network applications, and testing the functionality and control of the installed system.

Deliverable(s):

- Installed, operational network

Task 9: Install DBMS subsystems

The objective of this task is to install the DBMS subsystems according to vendor specifications. The task steps include installing the DBMS engine subsystem, installing the definition tools subsystem, installing the processing interface subsystem, installing the application development tools subsystem, and installing the data dictionary and data administration subsystem. The methodology for installing DBMS subsystems is summarized as follows.

Install the DBMS engine subsystem. The objective of this task is to install the DBMS engine subsystem that receives logical I/O requests from other subsystems and translates these requests into reads from and writes to database files.

Install definition tools subsystem. The objective of this task is to install the DBMS definition tools subsystem used to create the structure of the database (which includes the files, fields, relationships, constraints, overhead data structures, and other components of the database).

Install database access subsystem. The objective of this task is to install the DBMS access subsystem that allows users and programs to access the database system. All the database functions specified in the design are implemented by the processing interface system.

Install applications tool subsystem. The objective of this task is to install the applications tool subsystem which contains tools for developing application components such as forms, reports, and menus. The tools may also include program code generators.

Install data dictionary and data administration subsystem. The objective of this task is to install the data dictionary and data administration subsystem which performs query and report functions on the database metadata in addition to other roles. The data dictionary contains complete descriptions of the database structure and all the relationships among programs and data. The information in the data dictionary enables the data administrator to determine which records contain the data item; the forms, reports, and programs that use the data item; and security considerations.

Task 10: Implement the database

The objective of this task is to implement the database according to the relational models expressed in the design. The task steps include defining the database structure to the DBMS, allocating media space, and creating the database data. The methodology for implementing the database is summarized as follows.

Define the database structure to the DBMS.   The objective of this task is to define the relational designs to the DBMS. Some DBMS products require that the relational designs be defined in text format; others provide a graphical means for defining the structure of the database (e.g., Paradox).

Allocate media space.   The objective of this task is to allocate database structures to physical media. The specific tasks to be performed depend on the DBMS product used. Some DBMS products allocate space automatically. All that has to be done is to assign the database to a dictionary and give it a database name. Other products require that the distribution of the database data across disks and channels be carefully planned according to the nature of application processing.

Create the database data.   After defining and allocating the database to physical storage, the database data must be created. The methodology for creating database data depends on the specific application requirements and the features of the DBMS product selected for use. Some DBMS products have features and tools to readily facilitate importing the data from various media. Some require that all the data be entered manually (e.g., by keyboarding, or using applications programs created by the developers). After entering the data, all data must be verified regardless of the methodology used to create the database.

Task 11: Install application

The objective of this task is to install the new application. The task steps include either creating installation diskettes and installing the application on each machine, or distributing the application over the network. The approach used will depend on the facilities available and the number of clients and servers on which the application components must be installed.

Task 12: Perform acceptance tests

The objective of this task is to verify that the total system performs in the operational environment. All tests are conducted using the actual external interface. The results of the acceptance test should be compiled and published in a formal *acceptance test report* that presents an analysis of each test performed and summarizes the results of the completed acceptance test process. The test analysis segment of the report should identify each test case by name and number and analyze the performance of the system as tested compared to the criteria for successful completion as defined in the test plan specified during the internal design. The test summary segment of the report should summarize the capabilities demonstrated by the system, identify any deficiencies uncovered during the acceptance test, and summarize suggested refinements to improve the performance of the system, and reference the impact that such refinements would have on the design specifications.

Object-Oriented and Client/Server Resources

Part 3 of this book provides a listing of commercially available resources applicable to the design, development, and implementation of an object-oriented client / server computer system. The listing is not intended as a comprehensive guide. Information was derived from secondary research and a compendium of information resources developed by the author.

Chapter 7, Object-Oriented and Client/Server Resources, *identifies and describes object-oriented applications development systems, compilers and languages, programming utilities, and systems development methodologies.*

Chapter 8, Client/Server Resources, *identifies and describes network operating and database and file management systems that relate to the design of a client-server architecture.*

Chapter 9, Network Management Resources, *identifies and describes packages which can be used by the network administrator for management, monitoring, and reporting purposes.*

7

Object-Oriented Resources

This chapter identifies and describes many of the latest state-of-the-art objected-oriented products. The products listed are categorized as follows.

Applications development systems that facilitate object-oriented programming, screen design, program generation, debugging, testing, documentation, and reporting.

Compilers and languages that support the design and implementation of an object-oriented computing system.

Database and file management systems including query languages, dictionaries, tools and utilities, natural and fourth-generation languages, database performance analyzers, and database links.

Programming utilities that support the programming functions of an object-oriented system (including program standardization and optimization tools, cross-reference facilities, string and character handling, table maintenance, floating-point and array processors, assemblers, and linkers).

Systems development methodologies and CASE (computer-aided software engineering) tools which can assist in the control of large system development projects by means of an integrated approach to design. Integrated CASE software is included in this category.

Applications Development Systems

This section identifies and briefly describes some of the commercially available applications development packages that provide tools and aids for application design, implementation, and testing.

ART*Enterprise for Windows is a development tool that provides for rapid prototyping and deployment, object-oriented programming, built-in graphical user interfaces (GUIs) with multimedia capabilities, data integration and modeling from multiple DBMSs, event-driven and client/server open architecture, access to unstructured information, business rule processing with "what if" analysis, and business process reengineering and downsizing. (Inference Corp.)

ART-IM for Windows is an object-oriented, client/server application development tool that allows the user to build applications that apply judgment, policy, and business knowledge to generate assessments, recommendations, decisions, and explanations. Features include a point-and-click environment and a GUI class library. (Inference Corp.)

Async Professional is an object-oriented communications toolkit that enables a user to build asynchronous (async) applications. It includes ZMODEM protocol, data decompression tools, and object-oriented and procedural calling interfaces. Features include a multiwindow communications program with menus, text editor, and mouse support. It provides for the creation of time-stamped audit trails of all async interrupts and characters sent or received. (Turbopower Software.)

C++/Views provides an application development framework for building C++ cross-platform applications. It includes a C++ object class library and menu-driven class browser, C++/Browse. (Liant Software Corp.)

Choreographer for Windows is an object-oriented development environment for designing, implementing, delivering, maintaining, and managing mainstream corporate MIS (management information system) applications. It extends SmallTalk technology to include client/server, mainframe connectivity, and standard GUI team development. (Guidance Technologies, Inc.)

CommonBase is a collection of C++ classes for databases. It allows the user to develop applications using embedded SQL or proprietary applications programming interface (API). The package supports ANSI SQL Level 2 with extensions for referential integrity. The package provides kick-down functions that return low-level information needed to make direct calls to the host database system. It is portable between databases operating systems and compilers. (Imagesoft, Inc.)

Component Workshop is a graphical environment for C++ development. The package includes a C++ compiler and linker, memory management system, portable application framework, and C++ class library. It provides for browsing, editing, and debugging and allows developers to browse and edit class hierarchy and members of class. (Component Software Corp.)

Concurrent Referencer System (REF) is a menu-driven, Paradox-based application development environment for nonprogrammers, advanced developers, and corporate users. It creates entire applications, including system menus, multiuser editing, reports, help screens, lookup help, and graphics. (Ensemble Corp.)

Enfin/3PM is an object-oriented fourth-generation language (4GL) application development environment with a set of visual programming tools. It allows interactive development of user interfaces, reports, database front ends, and financial and mathematical models and generates object-oriented source code in ASCII format. Features include a point-and-click function that allows a user to link SQL database tables and queries with Enfin/3 screen forms and reports. (Enfin Software Corp.)

Envy/400 is an object-oriented application development environment that allows developers to create client/server applications combining CUA 91 object-oriented interfaces with AS/400 enterprise models. It includes a visual program generator for creating GUIs and host code facilities for developing applications. (Object Technology International, Inc.)

FACETS is an object-oriented 4GL development toolkit. FACETS generated applications are 100 percent portable and independent of databases. The package features graph view, direct manipulation of forms definitions, flexibility to manipulate screens and widgets, integration with SmallTalk's development environment, multiple key access, and expanded method library, and includes on-line, context-sensitive help. (Reusable Solutions, Inc.)

GainMomentun SQL Option is a set of object-oriented graphical tools for designing, implementing, and executing applications which interact with ANSI-SQL RDBMS. It eliminates the need to write code and allows developers to deliver applications that simultaneously interact with SQL databases from multiple vendors. (Gain Technology, Inc.)

Hood Toolset is a hierarchical object-oriented toolset that allows objects to have data and operations represented and processed. It provides for requirements analysis, design, and Ada code generation. The package consists of specification and design creation tools, interactive graphical and text editors, object management store, and output tools for code and document generation. (Caset Corp.)

Level5 Objects for Microsoft Windows is an object-oriented version of IBI's Level5 expert systems software that combines object-oriented techniques with multiple inferencing in a window-based environment. It features built-in system object classes that provide a new knowledge base with custom or predefined default system classes and logic tools. The package supports forward, backward, and mixed-mode inferencing. (Information Builders, Inc.)

LXEZ is an object-oriented application development tool to design programs for LXE radio-frequency data terminals. It separates user interface capabilities from object-dependent code using event-driven architecture. (Process Control Systems, Inc.)

Object for Windows is an object-oriented development language used to create new applications for Windows 3.1. It provides interfaces to SQL databases such as Microsoft SQL Server, IBM EE Database Manager, Oracle, and MDBS IV. Features include functions necessary to create elements of graphical applications such as buttons, list boxes, and menus. (Micro Data Base Systems, Inc.)

Object/1 is an object-oriented development language for creating new applications for OS/2 PM. The package provides interfaces to Microsoft SQL Server,

IBM EE Database Manager, Oracle, and MDBS IV. It creates elements of graphical application such as buttons, list boxes, and menus. (Micro Data Base Systems, Inc.)

Object/1 Professional Pack manages Oracle database sessions with Object/1 applications. Features include row buffering for queries, built-in Oracle forms login dialog, extended bitmap support, support for data type conversion, automated data transfer to and from Object/1 forms, and support for direct calls to Oracle Dynamic Link Library (DLL) Level 1 interface. (Micro Data Base Systems, Inc.)

ObjectCenter is a C++ programming environment for developing, debugging, testing, and maintaining C++ programs. It features advanced tool integration, error detection, testing capabilities, and accelerated turnaround program modifications. (CenterLine Software, Inc.)

Object/Development is an applications management tool that enables developers to manage all aspects of the development process. It includes tools for analysis and design, interface design, and project management. (Imagesoft, Inc.)

ObjectKit SmallTalk Advanced Programming for Windows is a companion product to ObjectWorks SmallTalk It includes performance analysis tools, programming tools, browsers and classes, parser compiler, and a terminal emulator communications facility. (ParcPlace Systems, Inc.)

Object PM is a C++ class library that builds OS/2 2.0 applications by providing prewritten code that can be extended by the programmer. It includes code for over 120 object types (including windows, icons, menus, event handling, and threads) and features a Forms Manager tool which allows programmers to build forms for OS/2 applications. (Raleigh Systems, Inc.)

ObjectWorks C/C++ is a C++ development environment that allows users to share code information. It facilitates creation of applications by integrating UNIX development utilities into the development environment. The package provides a cross-referencing utility. (ParcPlace Systems, Inc.)

ObjectWorks SmallTalk for Windows is an object-oriented development system that allows a user to create interactive, graphics-oriented applications. It includes facilities for dynamic compilation into native machine code, and provides over 400 types of portable objects and integrated development tools. (ParcPlace Systems, Inc.)

PowerClass is an object-oriented library for Powersoft's PowerBuilder. It includes standard Windows elements and encapsulated language scripts for building applications. (Serverlogic Corp.)

Prolog++ is an object-oriented Prolog application development environment that includes dynamic and static objects with attributes, functions, and methods; class hierarchies with single and multiple inheritance; public, private, and local methods; browsers to navigate object hierarchies; and daemons for data-driven programming. (Quintus Corp.)

Recital Fourth Generation Environment is an object-oriented development system that allows use of predefined objects and user-defined objects as building blocks. It allows for integration of 3GL, SQL, and other RDBMSs (relational database management systems). (Recital Corp., Inc.)

SmallTalk/V 286 is an object-oriented programming system. It provides color graphics, including a color palette window. It has an incremental program development capability and features overlapping windows and pop-up menus. The package supports as many objects as memory allows and includes more than 110 classes and 2000 methods. It provides object-oriented Prolog and integration with other languages via assembly language primitives. (Digitalk, Inc.)

SmallTalk/V DOS is an application development system that uses a relational database. Developed applications will transfer unaltered among many machine types. The package includes a screen builder, report writer, internal language, automatic documenter, and a run-time-only system and utility set. (Digitalk, Inc.)

SmartStar Vision is an object-oriented development system that integrates GUI objects with a set of general-purpose database objects in a single environment. Database objects include a set of methods that encapsulate all standard run-time SQL behaviors appropriate for each style of window system supports. Features include a multiple-SQL query optimizer and distributor that supports industry standard SQL database. (SmartStar Corp.)

Style for C++ is a class library that manages all associations and links between C++ objects and facilitates building any C++ application. The package provides for consistent paradigm, traversal functions, built-in traversal cycle protection, and built-in integrity checking. It supports object sequencing, multiple inheritance, recursive structures, user-defined condition handling, and dynamic memory management. (Software Ingenuities, Inc.)

Text Management Library is an object-oriented portable toolkit that lets a user produce text-based applications faster than is possible with conventional text-manipulation tools. It provides for building interactive applications that mix fonts and character sets and presents text on screen and hard-copy devices. The package supports all national languages and is consistent with National Language Support standard. (Hewlett-Packard Co.)

Tigre Programming Environment is an object-oriented system that speeds development of GUI applications and allows a user to run applications on a range of platforms without modification. It includes the Tigre interface Designer library of components used to build color GUIs such as buttons, text editors, picture viewers, and other commonly used interface items. (Tigre Object Systems, Inc.)

UniSQL/4GE ObjectMaster is an object-oriented application development and prototyping tool which allows users to develop customized, reusable GUI-based multimedia-enabled applications. It provides support for a variety of concurrency control protocols, data drilldown algorithms, multimedia data access, interwindow message parsing, and integration with existing non-UniSQL tools, applications, and network servers. The package includes ObjectMaster Editor and Application Folder. (ImoSQL, Inc.)

VZ Programmer is an application development environment providing C++ programmers with object-oriented programming, GUI toolkit, and extensible database to create classes and attach function to objects. Features include an object database, attribute editor, hierarchical grouping, compiler, debugger, browser and linker, ANSI C++ language, message and event handling, and a memory management system. (VZ Corp.)

XShell is a distributed object-oriented system development environment that allows a user to construct large-scale systems of cooperating programs distributed across networks of computers. It encapsulates software programs as software objects with an abstract interface and allows systems architects to handle programs as extensible building blocks with standard interfaces. (Expertsoft Corp.)

zAPP provides a framework for C++ development of Windows applications It encapsulates Windows API into C++ objects. The package provides a memory manager to avoid depleting the pool of global memory handles. It provides built-in support for selecting and configuring printers and features a dynamic message handling facility that can dispatch messages or ranges of messages to individual C++ member functions. (Imagesoft, Inc.)

Compilers and Languages

This section identifies and briefly describes some of the commercially available compiler and language products that support the development and implementation of an object-oriented computer system.

AIX XL C++ Compiler/6000 is an object-oriented programming language that provides capabilities of C language to allow the user to start from a familiar base and migrate to C++. The package includes a C++ compiler, a C++ class browser, a set of C++ class libraries, and a test coverage tool for the IBM RS/6000 family of processors. (IBM.)

Borland C++ for Windows is a C++ compiler that allows a user to build object-oriented Windows applications. It provides an integrated development environment with a professional editor based on BRIEF technology. The language features exception handling, templates for type safety and reusability, with a full run-time library. Also included is the Object Windows Library providing numerous windows objects and control elements, including full VBX support. It supports container classes for rapid software development, 16- and 32-bit compilers targetable to Windows 3.x, Win32s, Windows NT, DOS, DOS overlays, and NT console mode. It includes a GUI debugger, a project manager supporting multiple targets within a project, the AppExpert visual programming tools, and the ClassExpert supporting hierarchical event lists. (Borland International.)

EPC C++ is a compiler which adheres to language defined by ANSI Base Document and AT&T V.2.1 specification. (Migration Software Systems, Ltd.)

Green Hills C++ Cross and Native Compiler is an object-oriented C++ compiler for embedded system development. It supports embedded development environments for M680X0 and M88000 targets. (Oasys, Inc.)

Lucid C++ is a compiler that provides for global register allocation, global common subexpression elimination, global constant folding, redundant store elimination, loop induction variable elimination, strength reduction, code hoisting, tail recursion removal, instruction scheduling, and partial and total redundancy elimination optimizations. It includes shared and unshared libraries C++ debugging and other functions. (Lucid, Inc.)

NCR C++ is an object-oriented programming language that includes a multiple inheritance feature which allows classes of objects to inherit behavior from more than one other class of objects. (NCR Corp.)

NDP C/C++ 860 is a multidialect compiler that supports C++ specifications. It includes facilities for in-line assembly, full function in-liner, classes, single and multiple inheritance, constructors, destructors, and function and operator overloading. (Microway, Inc.)

Oregon C++/C Development System generates code and eliminates the need for translation from C++. It includes a source-level debugger, NIH OOPS class library support of shared libraries, and VAX C calling sequence. The software is compatible with AT&T's translator and task library. (Taumetric Corp.)

Pyramid C++ is a general-purpose object-oriented programming language that supports enhanced type checking and data abstraction. It includes an inheritance feature that enables code to be easily reused. It provides for program type conversion, operator and function name overloading, data hiding, type-safe linkage, constant and reference data types, in-line functions, and heap management. (Pyramid Technology Corp.)

SPARCworks Professional C++ includes SPARCompiler C++ optimizing compiler and SPARCworks toolset. It provides for C++ implementation and incorporates functionality of AT&T's translator. The package supports C++ templates, debugging of optimized code, ANSI C facilities, position-independent code generation, and name demangling. It includes a task library that enables simulation, control, and modeling of UNIX system processing in object-oriented paradigms. [Sunpro (unit of Sun MicroSystems, Inc.).]

Tier for Windows is a C++ object library for Windows. It includes over 90 classes which allow full access to Windows functionality, subclassing, dynamic link library (DLL), inter- and intraapplication object-to-object communications, model and modeless dialogs, and user-defined resources. (Sturmer Hauss Corp.)

TopSpeed C++ is a compiler that includes a code/data overlay system, multitasking support, integration into TopSpeed development environment, smartlinking, support for multiple memory models, segment-based points, full implementation of long doubles, and run-time error checking. (Clarion Software Corp.)

Turbo C++ Professional includes Turbo C++, Turbo Debugger, Turbo Profiler, and Turbo Assembler. It utilizes VROOMM (Virtual Run-Time Object-Oriented Memory Manager) and provides for overlapping windows, mouse support, multifile editor, dialog boxes, Smart Project Manager which allows file by file option settings, and context-sensitive hypertext help. (Borland International, Inc.)

Turbo Vision is a programming language product comprised of Borland's C++ compiler and Turbo Vision for C++ application framework that simplifies development of computer programs. It features a programmer's platform containing overlapping windows, mouse support, turbo help, multifile editor, and integrated debugger. (Borland International, Inc.)

Visual C++ is a compiler that features a class browser, code generator, integrated debugger, and resource editor. The compiler provides for hypertext linkage of output error messages and error code explanations with color syntax highlighting. (Microsoft Corp.)

XVT++ for Windows is an interface library that provides C++ bindings to existing XVT implementations. It allows users to compile C++ code and link code with the XVT++ library and the supporting system with which the user is developing. The package permits the XVT++ library to make calls to supporting XVT library. (XVT Software, Inc.)

Zortech C++ Compilers for Windows is an implementation of C++ language that provides an integrated environment to allow a developer to edit, compile, link, and debug. It supports object-oriented programming and has a multiple inheritance and type-safe linkage feature that allows developers to write Windows and Presentation Manager applications. (Symantec Corp.)

Database and File Management

This section identifies and briefly describes some of the commercially available database and file management products that support the development and implementation of an object-oriented computer system.

AccSys for Paradox is a family of libraries designed to give user access to data and index files for Borland's Paradox database. The package is PC-MS/DOS- and OS/2-compatible. (Copia International, Ltd.)

Business Objects gives each object a simple name that describes the business purpose of the data. The user combines objects to create query. Runs on PC-MS/DOS. (Business Objects, Inc.)

C-Data Manager (CDM) is an object-oriented programming and database development tool that provides persistent support for data objects. The package includes library functions which define object types and relationships at run time supporting a dynamic database schema. CDM combines a network database model with B-tree based ISAM (indexed sequential access method). Runs on Apple Macintosh-, DEC DECstation/ULTIRX-, Sun/SunOS-, OS/2-,

NeXT-, IBM RS/6000/AIX-, and PC-MS/DOS-compatible systems. (Database Technologies, Inc.)

C-Data Manager for Windows (CDM) is an object-oriented programming and database development tool that provides library functions which define object types and relationships at run time to support dynamic database schema, with persistent support for data objects. The package includes library functions which define object types and relationships at run time supporting a dynamic database schema. (Database Technologies, Inc.)

Distributed Object Database Management System enables the database to be accessed while changes are made at any site. Locking at object rather than page level allows schema modification and provides concurrent control. Runs on IBM RS/6000/AIX; HP Apollo Domain/Domain/OS, HP-UX; Sun/SunOS; Silicon Graphics; and DEC DECstation/UlTRIX. (Itasca Systems.)

Distributed Object Integration Tool (DOIT) is a distributed object management system that provides flexible architecture for distributed database access applications. The package is Sun/SunOS-compatible. (Object Systems Corp.)

GemStone is an object-oriented DBMS which allows multiple users to share large amounts of multimedia information. It stores objects permanently with database-style protection and access facilities. Runs on DEC VAV, MicroVAX, DECstation/MVS; MicroVMS, ULTRIX; Sun SPARstation/SunOS; IBM RT RS/6000/AIX; PC-MS/DOS; Apple Macintosh II; HP 9000 Series 700, and 7000/HP-UX. (Servio Corp.)

Greenleaf Database Library for Windows is a database library for C++ developers. It supports FoxPro 2 CDX files. The package is Windows 3.x-compatible. (Greenleaf Software.)

G-Base/GTX is an integrated object management system designed to support industrial hypermedia applications in transaction processing environments. It provides a language-independent, ANSI standard, client/server architecture for storage of graphics, images, voice, video, and other complex data types. Runs on DEC VAX/VMS-compatible platforms. (Object Databases.)

GTX Object Repository is a VAX/VMS database server used to support client workstation applications in a heterogeneous environment. It allows users to write applications in any computer language and utilize multiple-data models. It supports large multimedia databases, fault-tolerant network applications, archival of real-time data, and recall of temporal object versions required for group work and on-line backup. (Object Databases.)

IDB Object Database for Windows is a distributed object-oriented database programmable in ANSI C. It supports multiple inheritance, polymorphism, binding, transactions for concurrency control, versioning, linking, heterogeneous networks, and exceptions. The package is Windows 3.x-compatible. (Persistent Data Systems, Inc.)

KSC ChangeManager is a set of object-oriented utilities which extend source code maintenance mechanisms of SmallTalk. It requires ParcPlace Software's

ObjectWorks/SmallTalk. Runs on UNIX and is Apple Macintosh-compatible. (Knowledge Systems Corp.)

O2 System offers productivity during the design, coding, testing, and maintenance phases of applications development by integrating the O2 Engine and object-oriented DBMS with the application development environment and a set of GUI development tools. Runs on HP/HP-UX, Solaris; IBM RS/6000/AIX. (O2 Technology.)

Objectivity/DB is an object-oriented DBMS for applications that require data modeling, involve object relationship management, and demand performance in managing large amounts of data. Includes distributed schemas, on-line incremental backups, and restore. Objectivity/SQL++ for SQL-compliant ad hoc query interface, schema evolution, and object migration. Runs on DEC DECstation-, VAX/ULTIRX,VMS-, Sun-3-, AT&T UNIX System V-, IBM RS/6000 AIX-, HP 9000/HP-UX-, Silicon Graphics/IRIX-, and NCR 3000 compatible systems. Includes database administrative tools and program interfaces. (Objectivity, Inc.)

ObjectStore is an object-oriented database environment for C++. It provides distributed database functionality and offers a development environment for implementing large-scale applications and migration path for existing applications. Runs on IBM RS/6000/AIX, AT&T UNIX System V, Sun/Solaris, DEC/ULTRIX, NeXT, NCR 3000, and HP/HP-UX. (Object Design, Inc.)

ObjectStore for Windows is an object-oriented, C++-based DBMS for implementing large-scale, data-intensive design applications. It requires Borland C++ 3.0 or greater and Sun PC-NFS 3.5a or later. The package is Windows 3.x-compatible. (Object Design, Inc.)

Ontos DB is an object-oriented DBMS that allows users to build applications with outside C++ development tools. Runs on Sun-3,4, SPARstation/SunOS; IBM RS/6000/AIX; DEC DECstation/ULTRIX; and HP Apollo 9000l SCO UNIX. (Ontos, Inc.)

Ontos for OS/2 is an object-oriented DBMS that combines traditional database functions with object-oriented capabilities. It includes a distributed client/server architecture, translations, concurrency control, versioning, seamless C++ interface, SQL, graphical database administrator and browser, and open architecture. (Ontos, Inc.)

OpenODB is an object-oriented DBMS for building large multiuser and complex business applications. The system is designed to allow users to migrate to an object oriented environment while still accessing and using existing applications and data. It tracks data located in other databases or applications and returns information to the user in a standard form. Runs on HP 3000 and 9000 systems. The system supports multimedia, video, images, voice, and text. (Hewlett-Packard.)

Platinum Object Administrator manages QMF objects. It allows users to copy or move objects, optionally changing object name or owner. Runs on IBM/MVS/XA and MVS/ESA. (Platinum Technology, Inc.)

POET is an object-oriented DBMS that allows Aldus developers to extend capabilities of the application at run time without recompiling it. Runs on HP/HP-UX, SCO UNIX, 386/ix, NeXT, Apple Macintosh, OS/2, and Sun/SunOS. (POET Software.)

POET for Windows is an object DBMS that allows Aldus developers to extend capabilities of the application at run time without recompiling it. The package is Windows 3.x-compatible. (POET Software.)

Raima Object Manager is an object-oriented DBMS for C++ applications. It provides object persistence and object relationship management. Runs on PC-MS/DOS, DEC/ULTRIX, IBM/AIX, Sun/SunOS, OS/2, AT&T, and UNIX System V. (Raima Corp.)

Raima Object Manager for Windows is an object-oriented DBMS for C++ applications. It provides object persistence and object relationship management and encapsulates object storage and database navigation into C++ class definitions. The package is Windows 3.x-compatible. (Raima Corp.)

Serius Database is a component of the Serius Object Library that allows users to build multiuser databases. Provides database objects with tools for creating database systems with tables; layouts; and a full set of field types to construct flat-file or relational, single- or multiuser databases. Runs on Apple Macintosh Plus. (Serius Corp.)

SMARTstore is an object-oriented database of Procase's SMARTsystem. It supports the software development and maintenance processes. Runs on Sun-3, SPARstation/SUNOS, HP 9000/HP-UX, IBM RS/6000/AIX, and NCR System. (Procase Corp.)

Versant is an object DBMS that simplifies and accelerates design of complex applications for engineering, office automation, and computer-aided publishing markets. It includes class libraries, scheme generators, browsers, and database navigators. (Versant Object Technology.)

Versant Star is a software gateway that provides users of Versant's object database with access to data stored in Oracle's relational database during standard SQL statements. It supports C++. (Versant Object Technology.)

Programming Utilities

This section identifies and briefly describes some of the commercially available programming utilities that support the development of an object-oriented computer system.

application::ctor is a Windows-based C++ productivity tool that includes an object-oriented View Editor, a user interface class library containing over 100 classes, and a C++ browser. (Compass Point Software, Inc.)

A/UX Developer's Tool is a programmer's toolkit for A/UX application development that includes a C++ compiler, ResEdit resource editor, SADE source code debugger, MacsBug machine language debugger, and a library of source and object A/UX system calls. (Apple Computer, Inc.)

Btrv++ is a C++ class library that creates objects with its own directory. It allows objects to share the same Btrieve file in any mode and provides for implementation of Btrieve operations as member functions and for cloning files, iteration, file creation, extended operations, and multilocking. (Classic Software, Inc.)

C++ Data Structure Libraries is a library of persistent data structures (lists, trees, graphs, hashing, ER (entry relationship) models, and arrays which improve internal program design). The package includes a code generator. (Code Farms, Inc.)

C++/EMACS is a C++-based object-oriented programming tool. It includes facilities for syntax checking, control structure expansion, preprocessor macro expansion, on-line descriptions of C++ language key words, function names, and calling conventions. (Oasys, Inc.)

CBtrv for Windows combines C and C++ to produce a library with object-oriented capabilities. It provides support for all Btrieve operations and many value-added ones for file and index creation, extended operations, global Btrieve management, and error and event logging. (Classic Software, Inc.)

C-Clearly formats C++ source code into the user's preferred format. Style templates resemble C code that are edited to the user's exact style preference. (V Communications, Inc.)

C Developer's Toolkit contains 120 functions that allow programs to use the Emerald Bay database engine to store and retrieve data. It works with Borland's Turbo C and C++ and includes C database libraries, data browser program, database repair and log replay programs, and database administrator. (Emerald Bay Group.)

C Programmer's Toolbox contains over 30 tools for C and C++ program development, program analysis, file and data verification, and file and data filtering. It includes a source code beautifier, function analyzer, cross-reference generator, C semantic analyzer, performance profiler, and file directory archiver. (MMC AD Systems.)

C Programmer's Toolbox/MPW is a C++ programming tool that includes a source code beautifier and reformatter, cross-reference sequence checker, declaration translator, ANSI preprocessor, highlighter-printer, and a program organization reporter. (MMC AD Systems.)

C-scape is an object-oriented interface management system that includes a function library for programmers using C language. It includes a utility to produce C code. The library includes windowing, fields, menus, prompts, text editing, help, scrolling, full type support, definable validation, colors, and supports mouse and graphics. (Liant Software Corp.)

Classix is a C++ class library that provides 40 classes and 800 operations. It includes fully supported and reusable components, data structure, mathematical support objects, SmallTalk-like classes, and primitive data type mimics. (Vanguard Software.)

Cogent Prolog Toolboxes is a source and object code library that provides functions for interfacing with menus, backward chaining, object-oriented programming, frames, formatted I/O, DOS directory manipulation, and natural language. (Amziod.)

Comm++ is an object-oriented library for C++ that provides a hierarchy of classes to give developers access to and control of serial communications. It includes classes for Ymodem and Zmodem and supports Borland's C++. (Greenleaf Software.)

CBtrv combines C and C++ to produce a C library with object-oriented capabilities. It provides support for all Btrieve operations and many value-added ones for file and index creation, extended operations, global Btrieve management, and error/event logging. (Classic Software, Inc.)

CTRLCLIB-The Ctrl + C Library supports Borland C++ compilers. It allows programmers to set up interrupt handlers and traps to block keystroke combinations that would normally cause most programs to terminate unexpectedly. (Trendtech Corp.)

DBh++ is a C++ library that performs C++ interface to C APIs from leading RDBMS vendors. It develops object-oriented applications that use data and business rules incorporated in user's corporate information systems. (Rogue Wave Software, Inc.)

DynamicObject C++ is a Windows source code utility for C++ programmers. It consists of C++ source code which can be used to build a dynamic module, and includes C++ link list, memory management, drawing utility, mouse control method and data abstract, and virtual function and inheritance facilities. (GUI Computer, Inc.)

Energize Programming System (EPS) is an object-oriented programming environment with C/C++ compilers and GNU EMACS editor and debugger and other build-management tools. It includes browsers for language elements, errors, classes, and procedures calls, and provides interfaces for eventual integration of other programming tools. The package allows programmers to perform incremental compilation and navigate through an entire program to isolate problems. (Lucid, Inc.)

GFA-BASIC for DOS is a programming language which provides a C++ development environment. It contains more than 700 commands and functions and supports pointers, multidimensional arrays, windows-like, and GUI capabilities. (GFA Software Technologies.)

Linpack h++ is an object-oriented numerical C++ class library which includes FORTRAN algorithms. It provides solutions of systems of equations for many matrix types, solutions of over- and underdetermined systems of equations, and incremental least-squares solvers. (Rogue Wave Software, Inc.)

Loose Data Binder is a C++-consistent class library that provides a stack-queue-dequeue-list-array interface and built-in sort, search, and iterate functions. It can be saved on a stream for later reloading while multiple references to its elements are automatically resolved. (PSW/Power Software.)

Magic Fields is an object-oriented data field validation for Windows 3.x that provides predefined objects including numeric, text, alphanumeric, date, currency, phone number, and social security number. It offers support for international date and currency formats and eliminates coding data entry fields. (Blue Sky Software Corp.)

Matrix h++ is a C++ class library that includes general matrices, vectors, statistics, complex numbers, fast Fourier transformations, and specialized matrix classes, including banded, symmetric, positive-definite, hermitian, and tridiagonal. (Rogue Wave Software, Inc.)

Medley Programming Environment permits object-oriented, procedural, access-oriented, and rule-based paradigms to be used together with self-contained development, debugging, and run-time environment. It consists of an interactive window-based debugger, window-based inspectors, structure editors, source code manager, tools for application cross-referencing, and a meta-level workspace interface that supports user and developer task switching in windows applications. (Venue.)

MicroGA for Windows is a genetic algorithm toolkit for programmers that provides an object-oriented C++ framework of objects which can be applied to an array of problems (including simple function optimization and resource allocation). It includes a Galapagos code generator. (Emergent Behavior.)

ObjectChart C/C++ consists of C/C++ source code which builds real-time graphical objects. It includes the following facilities: line chart, linear or log-scaled axes, X-Y title and chart title, customized major and minor grids, scroll-bar control, movable legend and user-defined texts, and professional edition, including digitizer and zoom function. (GUI Computer, Inc.)

Object/Engineering for Windows is a C++ scientific class library that turns complex models into a collection of interacting objects. It provides facilities for numerical analysis, semipersistent containers, discrete-event simulation, exception handling, signal processing and time series, statistical tests, and random generators. (Imagesoft, Inc.)

Object Master is a multipurpose development tool for object-oriented programming. It provides a project window which specifies which source or resource files to include in the project browser window, a class tree which shows class hierarchy, a segment map that lists segments found through parsing source code, and a file map which displays methods in each corresponding source file. (ACIUS, Inc.)

Object Professional is a non-event-driven object-oriented library that provides text mode user interfaces such as text editors, menu systems, validated entry screens, file browsers, pick list, file selectors, and help systems. It is compatible with BC++, MSC/C++, and TC++. (Turbopower Software.)

ObjectTable C/C++ is a Windows source code utility for C/C++ programmers. It consists of C/C++ source code which can be used to build a multieditable list object. Features include multieditable column, automatic data validation, row and column title, cut-and-paste clipboard, and horizontal and vertical scroll. (GUI Computer, Inc.)

Object Threads for C++ is a C++ class library that provides for multithreading with standard C++ programs. It performs multiple asynchronous and concurrent operations such as built-in background printing and time updates to screen, disk operations, and user inputs. (Systems Assistance, Inc.)

Object Toolkit is an object-oriented toolkit for Turbo Pascal. It includes movable, scrollable, and stretchable windows, and base input field objects, providing string, integer, real-number, and date input, scrollable lists, radio buttons, check boxes, and memo field with word wrap. The package allows users to create linked lists with automatic sorting and pop-up and pull-down menus. It also includes a directory object for selecting single or multiple files and a system object to determine the computer hardware configuration. (Technojock Software, Inc.)

OORTK is an object-oriented multitasking real-time kernel for Turbo Pascal. It includes task and communication primitives defined as objects. The package provides dynamic task management, variable time slice, multilevel priority dynamic test scheduler, intertask communications, and resource sharing. (The Pixel Shoppe.)

PC Timer Objects is a rewrite or timer kernel designed to take advantage of C++ and Turbo Pascal Object language features. It provides services that support Borland C++, Microsoft C++, Turbo C++, and Zortech C++. (Ryle Design.)

QualBase is a collection of C++ class libraries providing multitasking, interrupts, arrays, strings, registers, stacks, binary trees, bit vectors, queues, conversions, hash tables, graphs, and list classes. It includes QOOPSM Qualware's extendable persistent store manager, array execution for speed, bounded array for debugging, and linked list modes for prototyping, as well as source code. (Qualware.)

Segment Consolidator converts large-model code to mixed-model code, deletes dead code, converts to register parameter passing, and supports Borland C++. (Optimite Systems.)

SQL*C++ for Windows is a developer's interface to C++. It allows programmers to perform joint queries in memory, create spreadsheets of tables in memory, run through tables, update columns repeatedly, and then store them in database. (Management Information Technology, Inc.)

SuperClass is an object-oriented programming utility for Clipper. It creates class libraries and objects and uses a send operator. The package provides for class definitions, constructor functions, single and multiple inheritance, protected and exported instance variables, and class methods and supports encapsulation and polymorphism. (Hallogram Software.)

Tools h++ is a C++ foundation class library that includes over 97 classes to handle strings, dates, times, files, Btree collections, link lists, queues, and stacks. It provides DDE (Dynamic Data Exchange) and clipboard stream buffer classes for data exchange with other applications while using stream I/O. (Rogue Wave Software, Inc.)

TransLibrary is an object-oriented class library designed to support development of logistics applications using graphical displays. It provides classes for definition and management of physical storage areas and classes that define physical items that can be placed into defined areas. (Transgraphics Systems, Inc.)

Turbo C Tools provides capabilities needed to write applications in Turbo C++. it features a windowing system that includes virtual, stackable menus and windows with optional borders and drop shadows, integrated mouse support, keyboard support, automatic hardware detection, and routines that allow a user to write ISRs (initiate-and-stay) and TSR (terminate-and-stay) programs. (Blaise Computing, Inc.)

VBtrv combines C, C++, and Visual BASIC to produce a library that brings object-oriented capabilities to Btrieve development under Visual BASIC. It provides position block, key buffer management, and other value-added features. (Classic Software, Inc.)

Windows System Library (Win/Sys) is a TPW, C, and C++ programming tool for Windows. It includes a set of string manipulation functions, date and time manipulation with international support, general-purpose data structures for bitsets, dictionaries, string tables, stacks, trees, and queues. (Turbopower Software.)

Zinc Application Framework is an object-oriented interface class library designed specifically for C++. It develops applications that run in true graphics and text mode and features pop-up and pull-down menus, scroll bars, toolbars, matrix, buttons, icons, string, date, numeric, and text fields. The package supports cut-and-paste operations. (Zinc Software, Inc.)

Systems Development Systems and Case Tools

This section identifies and briefly describes some of the commercially available systems development methodologies and CASE tools that support the development of an object-oriented computer system.

C++ Developer is a class construction and graphical browsing tool that allows users to create and maintain sophisticated C++ object-oriented programs. It graphically browses and edits classes and class inheritance hierarchies and checks consistency and design rules on program as it is being stored. (Hewlett-Packard Co.)

C++ Softbench is a C++ programming environment based on HP's SoftBench Framework. It integrates CASE tools to create a tailored environment. The package includes facilities for construction, text and support phases of software development with advanced C++ tools, and libraries of data abstraction components. It allows programmers to graphically view, construct, and edit classes and class hierarchies in C++. (Hewlett-Packard Co.)

Concourse-CASE is a CASE tool system which allows users to develop a data collection system using their own methodology. It provides immediate feedback about inconsistencies while in design phase and gives users a list of report and printing capabilities for documenting a developed solution. It also includes facilities for validating data collection solutions. (Intersoft Systems, Inc.)

HP VEE-Engine is an object-oriented software engineering tool that allows users to perform tasks by linking functional icons instead of writing lines of code. It enables users to select icons that direct the computer to generate, collect, analyze, or present data and then generate results. (Hewlett-Packard Co.)

HP VEE-Test is an object-oriented software engineering tool that allows users to perform tasks by linking functional icons instead of writing lines of code. It can be utilized in numerous computer-aided prototyping, experimentation, and test development applications. This package adds icons to HP's VEE-Engine which allows data collection for more than 170 HP instruments and other direct I/O elements. (Hewlett-Packard Co.)

IPSYS HOOD Toolset provides a hierarchical design method for deriving designs from expressions of requirements. It features Motif GUI support for real-time structured analysis, tracing and checking, design checking, management services, and dictionary browser and report facilities. (Ipsys Software.)

ISE Eiffel 3 is an object-oriented programming environment designed for large industrial projects. It consists of tools and reusable libraries, including EiffelBench, EffelVision, EffelBuild, EffelStore, EffelCase, and EffelBase. (Interactive Software Engineering, Inc.)

LANSA for Windows is a CASE tool that supports object-oriented design and prototyping, migration and reengineering, client/server architecture, portability, and interfaces to IBM's Advanced Applications. (LANSA USA, Inc.)

ObjectMaker for Windows is an object-oriented graphical software design tool that supports C++. C++ extensions include code generation and reverse-engineering capabilities. (Mark V Systems.)

ObjectModeler combines object-oriented analysis, design, and programming. It works over networks and has a collision-detection feature to reduce inconsistencies and duplication of entries when multiple users are at work. (Iconix Software Engineering, Inc.)

OMTool automates the process of preparing and updating object models. It provides for adding implementation details and generating data structures and class descriptions using GE's Object Modeling Technique. The package defines and manipulates relationships, aggregation, and generalization. (GE Advanced Concepts Center.)

Paradigm Plus for Windows is a configurable CASE tool that uses an object-oriented model to provide support to software engineering activities throughout the system life cycle. It allows users to use currently available paradigms or create their own CASE tools to support any paradigm or extension. (ProtoSoft, Inc.)

PRODOC Translator turns HLD Library language Flowforms into pseudo-code Flowforms in C++. (Scandura Intelligent Systems.)

Ptech consists of integrated and conceptual methodology, analysis, design, and prototyping tools, and a C++ code generator. It includes facilities that support concurrency, reusability, and hierarchical decomposition and allows objects to change classification. The package enables domain expert and end users to participate in the design using a natural vocabulary. It provides inference and constraint rules, a mathematical foundation, a graphical design tool, and an extensible metamodel. (Associative Design Technology.)

Rational Rose is a graphical object-oriented tool that lets developers perform language-independent analysis and design. It supports the Booch method, which lets developers move between analysis and design capabilities. It provides class browsers and also supports incorporation of reusable libraries such as Booch components. (Rational.)

Speedware is an object-oriented CASE and 4GL solution for on-line transaction processing (OLTP) applications. It includes Speedware/4GL with procedural and nonprocedural elements; Speedware/Designer CASE tool for designing, implementing, and maintaining systems with programming; and Speedware/Windows for producing consistent PC-like interface on standard ASCII terminals. (Speedware Corp.)

Teamwork/OOA and Teamwork/OOD provides a bridge between design and implementation in an object-oriented environment. It consists of a graphical editor and C++ code framework generator and an interface to Centerline's ObjectCenter C++compiler. The package generates data definitions associated with entities and relationships. (Cadre Technologies, Inc.)

TurboCASE is an object-oriented CASE tool for the analysis stage of software development. It allows for partitioning of large projects and provides merge function and import/export capabilities that allow sharing of project data. It also provides for real-time and structured modeling, modeling of project from up to 10 viewpoints, data-flow analysis, built-in consistency checking, and structured design support. (StructSoft, Inc.)

8

Client/Server Resources

This chapter identifies and describes various resources that relate to the design of the client/server architecture that must be integrated in the object-oriented environments discussed in previous chapters. The products listed are grouped as follows:

Network operating system products that enable the network administrator to monitor fault tolerance, locate a fault and confine its damage, and take corrective actions

Database and file management systems, including query languages, tools and utilities, database performance analyzers, and database links.

Client/Server Network Operating Systems

The following commercially available products provide the network operating software required to facilitate the flow of information between clients and servers:

BOS LAN is a local area network operating system that provides a user-transparent network structure. The system runs on PC-MS/DOS; DEC PDP-11, MicroPDP-11, VAX/VMS; Sun SPARCstation/SunOS; SCO UNIX; IBM RS/6000/AIX; NCR; HP9000; and Motorola 88000. (BOS National, Inc.)

ChosenLAN is a network operating system that supports Moses Computers' PromiseLAN. The system runs on PC-MS/DOS. (MOSES COMPUTERS, INC.)

DosTops is a peer-to-peer operating system that allows users to share resources across platforms. The system runs on PC-MS/DOS. (Sunselect.)

EasyNet NOS/2 Plus is a network operating system that provides remote spoolers, development toolkit, NetBIOS status utility program, and SAA CUA (common user access) interface. The system runs on PC-MS/DOS and OS/2. (Lanmark Corp.)

Everex-Web is a network operating system that allows users to share all network resources and optimize any station on network for use as a server for multiple applications or databases. The system runs on PC-MS/DOS. (Webcorp.)

Guardian 90 is a network operating system that allows incremental system expansion from a 2-processor to a configured 16-processor system. The system runs on Tandem NonStop II, TXP, EXT, CLX, VLX/Non-Stop-UX, and Guardian 90. (Tandem Computers, Inc.)

GV LAN/OS is designed for nontechnical users. It supports ARCnet, ethernet, and serial interfaces. The system runs on PC-MS/DOS. (Grapevine LAN Products.)

Hayes LANstep with LANstep Mail is a network operating system designed for small work groups. The system runs on PC-MS/DOS. (Hayes Microcomputer Products, Inc.)

InvisibleLAN is a peer-to-peer network operating system designed for use over industry-standard coaxial cable and twisted-pair wiring. The system runs on Windows 3.x and PC-MS/DOS. (Invisible Software, Inc.)

LAN Manager is a high-end operating system that provides a foundation for client/server computing and tools for the distributed administration of the network. The system runs on OS/2, PC-MS/DOS, and XENIX. (Microsoft Corp.)

LanMarc is a NetBIOS-based network operating system which operates on any NetBIOS adapter, including token ring, ARCnet, and ethernet. The system runs on PC-MS/DOS. (Network Development Corp.)

LAN Server Entry and Advanced is a network operating system based on Microsoft LAN Manager supporting most of its APIs. The system runs on OS/2 and PC-MS/DOS. (IBM.)

LAN Server Entry and Advanced for Windows is a network operating system based on Microsoft LAN Manager supporting most of its APIs. The system runs on Windows 3.x. (IBM.)

LANsmart is a network operating system for a D-Link LAN. The system runs on PC-MS/DOS. (D-Link Systems, Inc.)

LanSoft is a multilingual operating system that allows users to share files and resources. The system is PC-MS/DOS-compatible. (Accton Technology.)

LANtastic Network Operating System provides printer, disk, CD-ROM and file sharing, and e-mail and disk backup. The system is PC-MS/DOS-compatible. (Artisoft.)

MosesALL is a peer-to-peer network operating system that includes a network card and one copy of Moses NOS 3.0 network operating software. The system runs on PC-MS/DOS. (MOSES COMPUTERS, INC.)

Net/One LAN Manager is an OS/2 operating system that allows workstations and servers on Net/One to interoperate and share resources. The system runs on OS/2 and PC-MS/DOS. (Ungermann-Bass, Inc.)

Network-OS Plus is a multitasking operating system that provides a menu-driven user interface. The system runs on PC-MS/DOS. (CBIS, Inc.)

NET-1227 PC Network is a LAN operating system that connects PCs to network in a peer-to-peer architecture. The system runs on PC-MS/DOS. (Trans-M Corp.)

NetWare allows users to access all resources on the network. The network package runs on PC-MS/DOS, OS/2, Apple Macintosh, Sun SPARCstation/SunOS, HP Apollo, IBM RS/6000, SCO UNIX, and NeXT. (Novell, Inc.)

NetWare 386 is a LAN operating system that supports up to 250 users on one server. The system runs on PC-MS/DOS, Apple Macintosh and OS/2. (Novell, Inc.)

NetWare Lite is a peer-to-peer resource-sharing network operating system that provides network management, messaging, and local hard-drive sharing capabilities. The system runs on PC-MS/DOS. (Novell, Inc.)

NEX/OS Network Operating System features NetBIOS compatibility, security, remote access, power-off protection, on-line messages, calendar system, messaging system, spoolhandler, and print-driver and communication drive. The system runs on PC-MS/DOS. (DSC Communications Corp.)

NTNX is a network operating system that supports applications programs for Novell LANs. The system runs on PC-MS/DOS. (Alloy Computer Products, Inc.)

NOMAD is a fourth-generation relational database management system (4GL RDBMS) for developing standalone, cooperative, and client/server applications for end-user computing. It supports client/server access to Gupta's SQL Server in a LAN environment and Rdb and RMS in a VAX/VMS environment. The system runs on PC-MS/DOS. (MUST Software International.)

ODB/Server provides direct client/server access to DB2 for NOMAD users on DOS and OS/2 workstations. The system runs on PC-MS/DOS and OS/2. (MUST Software International.)

PathWay is a standards-based network operating system designed to link desktop computers with enterprise networks to form an internetworking system. The system runs on PC-MS/DOS, Apple Macintosh, DEC VAX/VMS, AT&T UNIX System V, and SCO UNIX. (Wollongong Group, Inc.)

QNX is a multiuser, multitasking, real-time distributed network operating system that runs in real mode or protected mode on all Intel-based micros. The system runs on PC-MS/DOS. (Quantum Software Systems, Ltd.)

SilverNET-OS a peer-to-peer networking operating system designed for small or medium-size businesses. The system runs on PC-MS/DOS, AT&T UNIX System V, and XENIX. (NET-Source, Inc.)

Sitka 10NET is a peer-to-peer network operating system that includes 10BEUI protocol which allows user to utilize Clipboard facility and chat with DOS and Windows users simultaneously. The system runs on PC-MS/DOS. (Sunselect.)

Sitka 10NET for Windows is a peer-to-peer network operating system for both DOS and Windows environments. (Sunselect.)

Solid LAN is a LAN operating system that includes a polling program which verifies that network stations are communicating with one another. The system runs on PC-MS/DOS. (Solid Technologies.)

Solid LAN-Windows is a network operating system that includes a polling program which verifies that the network stations are communicating with one another. The system runs on Windows 3.x. (Solid Technologies.)

StarGroup LAN Manager Server is the UNIX version of Microsoft's LAN Manager network operating system. The system runs on NCR Tower and AT&T UNIT System V. (NCR Corp.)

10Net is a peer-to-peer LAN operating system that provides print spool compression and print queue management. The system runs on PC-MS/DOS. (Tiara Computer Systems, Inc.)

3 + Share is a network operating system for dedicated or adapted PC LAN servers. The system runs on PC-MS/DOS and Apple Macintosh Plus SE,II. (3COM Corp.)

TotalNET for DOS is a LAN operating system that can be configured to act as a client, server, or combination server/client. The system runs on PC-MS/DOS. (Syntax, Inc.)

TSX-32 is a multiuser, multitasking network operating system that allows users of DEC 16-bit systems or DOS to migrate to Intel's 32-bit 80386 and 80486 architectures. The system runs on PC-MS/DOS. (S&H Computer Systems, Inc.)

VirtuOS 382 is a multiuser, multitasking network operating system that includes resource sharing. The system runs on PC-MS/DOS. (Microbase Information Systems Corp.)

VINES Unlimited is an integrated, distributed network operating system for local or global internetworking and management of the computers that constitute the network nodes. The operating system runs on PC-MS/DOS, OS/2, and Apple Macintosh. (Banyan Systems, Inc.)

VINES Unlimited for Windows is an integrated, distributed network operating system for local or global internetworking and management of the computers that constitute the network nodes. The operating system runs on Windows 3.x. (Banyan Systems, Inc.)

VOS (Virtual Operating System) is designed for transaction processing, networking, and multiprogramming in fault-tolerant environments. The system runs on Stratus/VOS. (Stratus Computer, Inc.)

Web for DOS is a peer-to-peer network operating system that provides basic file and printer sharing services. The system runs on PC-MS/DOS. (Webcomp.)

Web for Windows is a peer-to-peer network operating system that provides basic file and printer sharing services. The system runs on Windows 3.x. (Webcomp.)

Windows for Workgroups is a peer-to-peer network operating system which extends basic Windows utilities. The system runs on Widows 3.x. (Microsoft Corp.)

Database and File Management Systems

The following commercially available products provide the software required to manage or access server databases:

4D Server uses client/server architecture to provide a graphical administration environment that serves the structural components of databases and allows multiple clients to develop simultaneously. The system runs on Apple Macintosh. (ACIUS Inc.)

BlackSmith Open Net offers a client/server architecture for BlackSmith and other applications. It allows user interface operations and database operations to execute concurrently. The system runs on DG AviiON, HP 9000/HP-UX, IBM RS/6000/AIX, Prime, NCR, Sun/SunOS, Motorola, Pyramid, Sequent, and DEC VAX/VMS. (Stauffer Information Systems.)

CabNET is a network-based, front-end application for Microsoft's SQL Server. It allows users to store data files for most DOS and Windows-based applications in intuitive file folders. The system runs on OS/2 and Windows 3.x. (Imara Research Corp.)

CA-DATACOM/DAL Server allows Macintosh Data Access Language to have transparent access to CA-DATACOM databases via Macintosh interfaces. The system runs on Apple Macintosh and IBM/MVS/XA, MVS EMS. (Computer Associates International, Inc.)

CA-DB/PC CLIENT provides connectivity between PCs and CA-DB databases on VAX/VMS and UNIX. The system runs on PC-MS/DOS. (Computer Associates International, Inc.)

CA-IDMS/DAL Server allows Macintosh DAL users transparent access to CA-IDMS databases. It includes DAL client async operation, incremental compiler implementation, trace facility, utility for testing DAL program statements, and sample tables. The system runs on Apple Macintosh; IBM/MVS, MVS/XA, MVS/SP, MVS/ESA, VSE, VSE/SP, VSE/ESA, VM/CMS; DEC VAX/VMS; and AT&T UNIX. (Computer Associates International, Inc.)

CB-DB/DAL Server provides Macintosh DAL to have transparent access to CA-DB databases. It performs query and update functions and includes async operation with incremental compiler implementation, True compiler, and ANSI Standard SQL. The system runs on Apple Macintosh and IBM/MVS/XA, MVS EMS. (Computer Associates International, Inc.)

DataPrism is a front-end tool for SQL databases that can access Oracle database servers and all servers supported by Apple's DAL. The system runs on Apple Macintosh/System 7. (Brio Technology, Inc.)

DB/Advisor is a client/server application that provides extensions and front-end to Adager Corporation's Adager and other database maintenance tools. The system runs on Windows 3.x. (Leetech Software, Inc.)

DEC Access Works is a server family for information integration. It provides desktop access to DB2, IMS, VSAM, Oracle, Rdbb, RMS, and other databases. The system runs on DEC VAX/ULTRIX and Sun/SunOS. (Digital Equipment Corp.)

Entity Relational Database is a client/server product designed as a real-time alternative to conventional RDBMSs for use in applications. It allows data to be inputted from devices or in SQL. The system runs on DEC VAX/VMS, ULTRIX, HP/HP-UX, SCO UNIX, and Stratus. (Automated Technology Associates.)

FairCom SQL Servers are multithreaded database servers designed for developers who demand control of Oracle, Sybase, Novell, Gupta, Microsoft, and other SQL databases. The system runs on PC-MS/DOS, AT&T UNIX System V, SCO UNIX, 386/iX, Sun SPARCseries/SunOS, IBM RS/6000/AIX, and OS/2. (Faircom Corp.)

HyBase is a networkable SQL object-oriented database that allows users to create tables using such SQL operators as Select. It includes user-defined classes of objects as well as graphics. The system runs on Apple Macintosh. (Answer Software Corp.)

InfoPump is client/server middleware that "pumps" data and metadata between major databases on OS/2, UNIX, and mainframe platforms. The system runs on Windows 3.x and OS/2. (Trinzic Corp.)

Open Server for CICS allows SQL Server databases to access data, applications, and services from CICS and allows applications running under CICS to be invoked. The system runs on DEC VAX/VMS, IBM/MVS, and AT&T UNIX. (Sybase, Inc.)

Oracle Card is a multimedia, end-user database. It enables programmers to build front-end applications for the Oracle client/multiserver system. The system runs on Apple Macintosh SE,II. (Oracle Corp.)

Parley supports client/server communications. It automatically manages multiple, simultaneous server-to-client sessions. The system runs on Apple Macintosh, PC-MS/DOS, and DEC VAX/VMS. (Dome Software Corp.)

PC/Focus-MultiUser is a database server for OS/2 LANs. It supports 4 to 32 users. (Information Builders, Inc.)

PC/Focus SQL Server Interface enables Focus applications running on PC to transparently access data residing in the SQL Server. The system runs on PC-MS/DOS and OS/2. (Information Builders, Inc.)

Platinum Integrator is a transaction server for PC SQL Access to 3270 legacy applications. The system runs on IBM/VMS/ESA. (Platinum Technology, Inc.)

Recital/RDBserver allows users to integrate Rdb data on VAX with data from Recital databases residing on VAX and other computers. The system runs on DEC VAX, MicroVAX/VMS, ULTRIX, XENIX, and IBM/AIX. (Recital Corp., Inc.)

Recital/RMS Server allows users to integrate RMS data on VAX with data from Recital databases residing on VAXs and other computers. The system runs on DEC VAX, MicroVAX/VMS, ULTRIX, XENIX, and IBM/AIX. (Recital Corp., Inc.)

SequelLink Client/Server MiddleWare is a set of client- and server-based software components that provide Windows, Macintosh, UNIX, and OS/2 applications with direct access to host-based data and services across a wide range of industry-standard networks. The system runs on Windows 3.x, OS/2, Apple Macintosh, Sun SPARCstation/SunOS, IBM mainframe, AS/400 RS6000/MVS, OS/400, AIX, HP 9000/HP-UX, and DEC/ULTRIX. (TechGnosis, Inc.)

SQL Access Server for Rdb/VMS enables SQL Access client applications on any platform to perform read-write access to data in any Rdb/VMS database on the network. The system runs on DEC VAX, VAX-11, VAXft, MicroVAX, VAXstation, and VAXserver/VMS. (Digital Equipment Corp.)

SQL Administrator allows users to manage multiple SQL Server systems including remote sites from a single workstation. The system runs on OS/2. (Microsoft Corp.)

SQLBase Server is an SQL distributed DBMS for LANs that includes an editor, debugging facilities, and OLTP support. The system runs on OS/2, PC-MS/DOS, and Sun-4, and SPARCstation/SunOS. (Gupta Corp.)

SQLFile is a tool for manipulating data stored in SQL database servers. It facilitates data access directly from tables or through views. The system is PC-MS/DOS- and OS/2-compatible. (Gupta Corp.)

SQL Gateway/Oracle offers connectivity to any DOS, Windows, or OS/2 client on a PC LAN. The system runs on OS/2 and PC-MS/DOS. (Gupta Corp.)

SQL Gateway/Oracle for Windows Client enables graphical Microsoft Windows and OS/2 PM applications to access Oracle DBMS data anywhere in the enterprise. The system runs on Windows 3.x. (Gupta Corp.)

SQL Lite is a command-driven SQL processor that accepts virtually any SQL statement, including SELECT statements. The system runs on IBM AS/400/OS400. (Cozzi Research.)

SQL Multimedia for DEC Rdb manipulates, stores, and retrieves multimedia objects from client applications that work with VAX Rdb/VMS databases. The system runs on DEC DECsystem, DECstation, VAX, VAXstation, VAXserver, MicroVAX/OpenVMS, ULTRIX, PC-MS/DOS, and Apple Macintosh. (Digital Equipment Corp.)

SQL Router/Oracle provides connectivity to any DOS, Windows, IBM AS/400, or OS/2 client directly connected to an Oracle host. The system runs on OS/2, PC-MS/DOS, and IBM AS/400. (Gupta Corp.)

SQL Router/SQL Server offers Sybase SQL connectivity from any OS/2 client to UNIX or VMS host. The system runs on OS/2. (Gupta Corp.)

SQL Server runs multiple server applications with active data sharing between SQL Servers or between SQL Server gateways. The system runs on OS/2. (Microsoft Corp.)

SQL Server for NetWare provides NetWare users with access to a variety of SQL DBMSs. It utilizes server-to-server remote procedure calls (RPCs) to permit Sybase users on NetWare to talk to Sybase databases running on other platforms. The system is PC-MS/DOS-compatible. (Sybase, Inc.)

SQL Server for PC UNIX is a UNIX version of the SQL Server database. (Sybase, Inc.)

SQLWindows for OS/2 creates SQL-based applications for the OS/2 environment. The system includes a graphics form and an outline editor. Object functions allow multiple programmers to work on the same application simultaneously. (Gupta Corp.)

Vortex Client and Vortex Server allows applications to access data on different platforms over one or more network configurations without any reprogramming or additional hardware. The system runs on DEC VAX/VMS, AT&T UNIX System V, SCO UNIX, 386/ix, PC-MS/DOS, OS/2, and HP/MPE/XL. (Trifox, Inc.)

Xbase/Server is a client/server DBMS designed specifically for developers working in Xbase languages like FoxPro of Clipper. It runs on PC-MS/DOS, OS/2, and Apple Macintosh. (Megabase, Inc.)

9

Network Management Resources

As indicated in Chap. 2, network management consists of configuring, monitoring, controlling, and analyzing the resources available in the network; optimizing the use of those resources; and preventing and solving user problems. The network administrator is responsible for coordinating and integrating these activities. Toward this end, commercially available software packages are often acquired to facilitate the network management process. This chapter identifies and describes many of the latest state-of-the-art network management resources The products are listed by the management functions they support, specifically:

Fault management products that enable the network administrator to monitor fault tolerance, locate a fault and confine its damage, and take corrective actions

Configuration management products that assist the network administrator in controlling the network hardware, firmware, and operating systems

Performance management products that enable the network administrator to evaluate the network's reliability and level of performance

Security management products that provide tools for the management of security and the authorization of users to access network resources

Fault Management Products

The following commercially available products may be acquired to assist the network administration in fault detection, diagnosis, and correction:

5025 Network Management Center provides an integrated set of monitoring and diagnostic capabilities and information to isolate faults and maximize network performance. The package is Sun SPARCstation/SunOS-compatible. (Retix.)

Codeman AllNet Enterprise Network Manager gathers fault diagnostics and network traffic statistics. The package is Sun SPARCstation/SunOS-compatible. (Codenoll Technology Corp.)

Comsphere 6700 Dial Network Management System provides tools for fault isolation utilizing various diagnostic tests. The package is Windows 3.x-compatible. (AT&T Paradyne.)

DataPipe provides for configuration monitoring, performance monitoring, and fault detection. The package is Sun SPARCstation/SunOS-compatible. (Digitalk.)

DECmcc Fault Diagnostic Package provides a troubleshooting tool designed for isolating and resolving Transmission Control Protocol/Internet Protocol (TCP/IP) network problems. The package is DEC DECsystem-, DECstation-, VAX-, MicroVAX-, VAXstation-, VAXserver/ULTRIX-, and OpenVMS-compatible. (Digital Equipment Corp.)

DSM/Problem Manager tracks new and recurring network problems. The package is Tandem NonStop-compatible. (Tandem Computers, Inc.)

Expert Sniffer Analyzer identifies problems, makes diagnoses, and offers explanations on how to remedy problems. The package is PC-MS/DOS-compatible. (Network General Corp.)

GlobalView Software provides diagnostics for dial-up data communications networks. It configures and monitors modems from a single location regardless of modem location. The package is PC-MS/DOS-compatible. (UDS Motorola.)

HP OpenView Interconnect Manager provides configuration, fault diagnostic, and performance management capabilities for hubs, bridges, and routers in TCP/IP AppleTalk. The package is HP 9000-, AT&T UNIX System V-, and PC-MS/DOS-compatible. (Hewlett-Packard.)

Integrity System Management Suite is an object-oriented fault management system. The package is Tandem Integrity/NonStop-UX-compatible. (Tandem Computers, Inc.)

Isis Reliable Network File System (Isle RNFS) adds fault tolerance to NFS configuration with no changes required to application software of NFS file systems. The package is Sun/SunOS-compatible. (Isis Distributed Systems, Inc.)

ISOcomm Network Monitor assists in fault detection, troubleshooting, and maintenance. The package is PC-MS/DOS-compatible. (Modicon International.)

LANSafe II for Novell NetWare with Microsoft Windows is a fault-tolerant LAN auditing system. The package is Windows 3.x-compatible. (Network Security Systems, Inc.)

LAN Server Watch monitors and troubleshoots LAN servers. The package is Windows 3.x-compatible. (Brightwork Development, Inc.)

LANSight Support provides real-time configuration information from remote locations, diagnostic and monitoring capabilities, and security support. The package is PC-MS/DOS-compatible. (Intel Corp.)

LANView identifies malfunctioning stations. The package is PC-MS/DOS-compatible. (Cabletron Systems, Inc.)

MacPing analyzes network performance and helps users locate segments of the network having problems. The package is Apple Macintosh-compatible. (Dartmouth College.)

Management Station allows users to diagnose and correct system faults and bottlenecks. The package is DEC DECstation-, DECsystem-, VAX/VMS-, ULTRIX-, SCO UNIX-, Sun-3-4-, SPARCstation/SunOS-, and SCO Open Desktop-compatible. (Wollongong Group, Inc.)

MultiSMART Manager performs diagnostics and reports faults to enable early detection and correction of network problems. The package is PC-MS/DOS-compatible. (Kentrox Industries, Inc.)

NAMS provides automatic fault detection and alarming, password access, log printer and audit trail, network inventory data files, and a trouble-ticketing system. The package is DEC VAX/VMS-compatible. (CXR Dialog, Inc.)

NCRNet Manager provides an integrated set of management software: fault management, performance management, and configuration management. The package is NCR Tower-, OS/2-, PC-MS/DOS-, and AT&T UNIX-compatible. (NCR.)

NetPatrol Pack prioritizes problems with alarms highlighting malfunctioning servers and bridges. The package is Apple Macintosh-compatible. (The AG Group, Inc.)

Netsight Professional Enhancement monitors performance, errors, and security. The package is PC-MS/DOS-compatible. (Intel Corp.)

NetVisualizer is a network diagnostic tool. The package is Silicon Graphics RIX- and AT&T UNIX System V-compatible. (Silicon Graphics, Inc.)

NetWare Communications Services Manager configures, monitors, and maintains Network communication services anywhere on the network. Provides real-time alert reception, session control, and fault and performance measurement. The package is Windows 3.x-compatible. (Novell, Inc.)

NIMS (Network Information Management System) manages data equipment inventories, network configurations, system changes, and problem solving. The package is DEC VAX-, MicroVAX/VMS-, and IBM RS/6000/AIX-compatible. (Professional Computing Resources.)

OpenNet OSI Network Management includes facilities for performance, fault reporting, and security management. The package is AT&T UNIX System V-compatible. (Pyramid Technology Corp.)

OS/Eye*Node provides for configuration management, troubleshooting, and performance analysis. The package is IBM RS/6000/AIX-, DG AViiON/DG/UX-, HP/HP-UX-, SCO UNIX-, Sun/SunOS-, AT&T UNIX System V-, and DEC/OSF/1-compatible. (Digital Analysis Corp.)

Remote LANView/Windows identifies malfunctioning stations and provides audio alarms. The package is Windows 3.x-compatible. (Cabletron Systems, Inc.)

StarGroup NetView Management Interface collects fault-tolerant information from AT&T's Network Manager, Router Manager, and Computer Manager and forwards alarms to IBM NetView management systems. The package is NCR Tower-, and AT&T UNIX System V-compatible. (NCR.)

Symmetry provides fault-resilient capability to PICK networks. The package is PICK-compatible. (Alpha Microsystems.)

Systems Monitor/6000 provides for fault and performance management. The package is IBM RS/6000/AIX-compatible. (IBM.)

TalkManage provides configuration, performance, and fault management. The package is Apple Macintosh-compatible. (The Distributed Technologies Corp.)

Time/View Integrated Management System provides for fault isolation and correction. The package is Sun SPARCstation/SunOS-compatible. (Ascom Timeplex, Inc.)

TokenVision is a real-time traffic monitoring system that monitors token ring traffic activity and network errors. The package is PC-MS/DOS-compatible. (TriCom.)

Uni-VIEW NMS is a graphics-based configuration management and fault isolation program. The package is PC-MS/DOS-compatible. (IBM.)

Configuration and Inventory Management Products

The following commercially available products can be acquired to assist the network manager in determining and controlling the hardware, operating system, and network configurations of the workstations on the network:

Argus/n monitors hardware and software status, configuration, and activity of up to 25,000 workstations on NetWare. The package is PC-MS/DOS-compatible. (TriCom.)

Argus/n InterNetwork monitors status, configuration, and activity of all workstations connected to a set of internetworked NetWare LANs. The package is PC-MS/DOS-compatible. (TriCom.)

AT&T Automatic Configuration Emulator automates the process of configuring and maintaining the Amdahl Network Administrator. The package is Amdahl/UTS-compatible. (AT&T.)

Command-Trac SNMP Network Management Station Software monitors, controls, and reconfigures large networking systems from centralized or remote network management stations. The package is Sun SPARCstation/SunOS-compatible. (AMP, Inc.)

DataPipe provides for configuration monitoring, performance monitoring, and fault detection. The package is Sun SPARCstation/SunOS-compatible. (Digitalk.)

DECnet/SNA Gateway Management provides configuration management capabilities for use with DECnet/SNA Gateway-ST and DECnet/SNA Gateway-CT products. The package is DEC VAX MicroVAX-, VAXstation/VMS-, and Micro/VMS-compatible. (Digital Equipment Corp.)

Enterprise Network Manager includes performance and configuration management facilities. The package is Sun SPARCstation-compatible. (Zenith Electronics Corp.)

GlobalView Software provides diagnostics for dial-up data communications networks. It configures and monitors modems from a single location regardless of modem location. The package is PC-MS/DOS-compatible. (UDS Motorola.)

GraceLAN is a network inventory tool that enables users to extract information on an AppleTalk network. It provides configuration, performance, and fault management. The package is Apple Macintosh-compatible. (Technology Works, Inc.)

GraceLAN Asset Manager tracks hardware and software components of a network. The package is Apple Macintosh-compatible. (Technology Works, Inc.)

History Analyzer tracks network configuration changes and creates baselines that help network managers schedule configuration changes at times they are least likely to interrupt the workflow. The package is HP/HP-UX-compatible. (Hewlett-Packard Co.)

HP OpenView Interconnect Manager provides configuration, fault diagnostic, and performance management capabilities for hubs, bridges, and routers in TCP/IP AppleTalk. The package runs on HP 9000, AT&T UNIX System V, and PC-MS-DOS. (Hewlett-Packard Co.)

Info-Power provides a tool for keeping records of vendor contracts and configuration management. The package runs on Sun SPARCstation/SunOS, DEC DECstation/&ULTRIX, HP Apollo 9000 Series 700/HP-UX, and IBM RS/6000/AIX. (Applied Innovation Management, Inc.)

Lan Automatic Inventory is a configuration system which creates LAN equipment databases. The package runs on PC-MS/DOS and Apple Macintosh. (Brightwork Development, Inc.)

Lan Automatic Inventory for Windows is a configuration system which creates LAN equipment databases. The package is PC-MS/DOS- and Apple Macintosh-compatible. (Brightwork Development, Inc.)

LANExam Node Agent monitors hardware inventory and system software configurations. The package is PC-MS/DOS-compatible. (Network Computing, Inc.)

LANExam Node Agent for Windows monitors hardware inventory and system software configurations. It stores and tracks configuration of NetWare workstations and servers. The package is Windows 3.x-compatible. (Network Computing, Inc.)

LANScan serves as a vehicle for monitoring inventory and configuration management. The package is PC-MS/DOS-compatible. (Vycor Corp.)

LANSight for Windows provides real-time configuration information from remote locations. The package is Windows 3.x-compatible. (Intel Corp.)

LANSight Support provides real-time configuration information from remote locations, diagnostic and monitoring capabilities, and security support. The package is PC-MS/DOS-compatible. (Intel Corp.)

Montage provides for device configuration management and access security. The package is Windows 3.x-compatible. (Octocom Systems, Inc.)

NAMS provides automatic fault detection and alarming, password access, log printer and audit trail, network inventory data files, and a trouble-ticketing system. The package is DEC VAX/VMS-compatible. (CXR Dialog, Inc.)

NCRNet Manager provides an integrated set of management software: fault management, performance management, and configuration management. The package runs on NCR Tower, OS/2, PC-MS/DOS, and AT&T UNIX. (NCR.)

NetKeeper is a configuration file manager capable of restoring a workstation to a stable configuration. The package is PC-MS/DOS-compatible. (Multima Corp.)

NetKeeper for Windows is a configuration file manager that provides an inventory of applications software and hardware components. The package is Windows 3.x-compatible. (Multima Corp.)

NetMapper is an integrated network management system that provides for configuration management and performance management. The package is Sun SPARCstation/SunOS- and PC-MS/DOS-compatible. (Intelligent Network Applications.)

NetWare Communications Services Manager configures, monitors, and maintains Network communication services anywhere on the network. Provides real-time alert reception, session control, and fault and performance measurement. The package is Windows 3.x-compatible. (Novell, Inc.)

Network Server Management System configures, controls, and monitors TyLink's Network Servers. The package is PC-MS/DOS-compatible. (Tylink Corp.)

NIMS (Network Information Management System) manages data equipment inventories, network configurations, system changes, and problem solving. It interfaces existing monitoring and diagnostic equipment. The package runs on DEC VAX, MicroVAX/VMS, and IBM RS/6000/AIX. (Professional Computing Resources.)

Open Management System (OMS) includes configuration and performance management utilities. The package is Sun SPARCstation/SunOS-compatible. (VitaLink Communications Corp.)

OS/Eye*Node provides for configuration management, trouble shooting, and performance analysis. The package runs on IBM RS/6000/AIX, DG AViiON/DG/UX, HP/HP-UX, SCO UNIX, Sun/SunOS, AT&T UNIX System V, and DEC/OSF/1. (Digital Analysis Corp.)

OSI 830 Global Network Management System is a network security and configuration support system The package is PC-MS/DOS-compatible. (Octocom Systems, Inc.)

Polycenter Extended LAN Manager configures, monitors, and observes any LAN Bridge, DECbridge, and DECconcentrator 500 media variant in an Extended LAN and FDDI (fiber-distributed data interface) network environment. The package runs on DEC DECsystem, DECstation, VAX, MicroVAX, VAXstation, VAXserver/ULTRIX, and OpenVMS. (Digital Equipment Corp.)

Polycenter System Census provides capability for gathering and displaying system configuration information. The package runs on DEC VAX/OpenVMS, ULTRIX, and PC-MS/DOS. (Digital Equipment Corp.)

Product Configuration provides configuration management control of software, hardware, and documentation. The package runs on DEC VAX, MicroVAX, VAXstation, VAXserver, DECstation/Open VMS, ULTRIX; Sun SPARCstation/SunOS; and HP 9000 Series 700/HP. (Digital Equipment Corp.)

Softstone Network Library is a configuration manager utility. The package is PC-MS/DOS-compatible. (Softstone Systems, Inc.)

SOLVE: Configuration manages objects, resources, and relationships with system and network. The package runs on IBM/MVS/ESA, MVS/SP, DOS/VSE, MVS/XA, and VM/ESA. (Systems Center, Inc.)

TalkManage provides configuration, performance, and fault management. The package is Apple Macintosh-compatible. (The Distributed Technologies Corp.)

TeMIP provides off-the-shelf fault management functions. The package is DEC VAX-, MicroVAX-, VAXstation-, and VAXserver/OpenVMS-compatible. (Digital Equipment Corp.)

Uni-VIEW NMS is a graphics-based configuration management and fault isolation program. It includes security sign-on, icon-based configuration, multi-window view, and real-time alarm processing. The package is PC-MS/DOS- and OS/2-compatible. (DSC Communications Corp.)

VINES Automatic Inventory gathers server and data configuration data when users log on each day. The package is PC-MS/DOS- and Apple Macintosh-compatible. (Brightwork Development, Inc.)

XNETMON Manager provides configuration management, and performance management facilities. The package runs on AT&T UNIX System V; Sun/SunOS; DG/DG/&X; SCO UNIX; DEC VAX/VMS, ULTRIX; and 386/ix. (SNMP Research, Inc.)

Performance Management Products

The following commercially available products can be acquired to assist the network manager in evaluating the system's reliability and level of performance.

18225 decNET Performance Analyzer provides real-time analysis of node performance and traffic characteristics. The package runs on DEC VAX, VAXstation, DECsystem/VMS, and ULTRIX. (Hewlett-Packard Co.)

5025 Network Management Center provides an integrated set of monitoring and diagnostic capabilities and information to isolate faults and maximize network performance. The package is Sun SPARCstation/SunOS-compatible. (Retix.)

5612 Mainstreet Network Planning Tool evaluates network performance and cost-effectiveness. The package is PC-MS/DOS-compatible. (Newbridge Networks Corp.)

Acct*Proxy collects performance data. The package runs on IBM RS/6000/AIX, DG AViiON/DG/UX, HP/HP-UX, SCO UNIX, Sun/SunOS, AT&T UNIX System V, and DEC/OSF/1. (Digital Analysis Corp.)

Bestnet Boundary Product analyzes and predicts response times, utilizations, and throughput. The package runs on IBM 370, 30XX, 43XX, and ES/9000/MVS/TSO. (BGS Systems.)

CA-MAZDAMON collects performance data for every component on the entire VTAM (virtual telecommunications access method) network. The package is IBM/VSE/ESA-, MVS/ESA-, and MVS/XA-compatible. (Computer Associates International, Inc.)

DataPipe provides for configuration monitoring, performance monitoring, and fault detection. The package is Sun SPARCstation/SunOS-compatible. (Digitalk.)

Enterprise Network Manager includes performance and configuration management facilities. The package is Sun SPARCstation-compatible. (Zenith Electronics Corp.)

HP OpenView Interconnect Manager provides configuration, fault diagnostic, and performance management capabilities for hubs, bridges, and routers in TCP/IP AppleTalk. The package runs on HP 9000, AT&T UNIX System V, and PC-MS-DOS. (Hewlett-Packard Co.)

MacPing analyzes network performance and helps users locate segments of the network having problems. The package is Apple Macintosh-compatible. (Dartmouth College.)

NCRNet Manager provides an integrated set of management software: fault management, performance management, and configuration management. The package runs on NCR Tower, OS/2, PC-MS/DOS, and AT&T UNIX. (NCR.)

NetMapper is an integrated network management system that provides for configuration management and performance management. The package is Sun SPARCstation/SunOS-, and PC-MS/DOS-compatible. (Intelligent Network Applications.)

NetMetrix NFS Monitor monitors traffic and performance by the server/client. The package is Sun SPARCstation/SunOS-compatible. (Metrix Network Systems, Inc.)

NetSaver is a network performance manager that allows user sites to edit VTAM tables while the network continues to function uninterrupted. The package is IBM/MVS/XA-, MVS/SP-, and VTAM-compatible. (Allen Systems Group, Inc.)

NetSECURE is a performance diagnostic tool that simulates backup and measures feed rate or performance of data. The package is PC-MS/DOS-compatible. (Tallgrass Technologies Corp.)

Netsight Professional Enhancement monitors performance, errors, and security. The package is PC-MS/DOS-compatible. (Intel Corp.)

NetSpy provides complete end-to-end network performance and response time monitoring. The package runs on IBM 370, 43XX, 30XX/MVS, MVS/XA, MVS/ESA, MVS/370, VM/XA SP, VM/SP, and VM/HPO. (Legent Corp.)

NetTester/1 provides network planning, benchmarking, testing, troubleshooting, and maintenance. The package runs on IBM 30XX, 43XX/MVS/XA/ESA, and PC-MS/DOS. (Phoenix Software International.)

NetView Performance Monitor collects, analyzes, and graphically displays behavior characteristics of a telecommunications network. The package is IBM/VM-, and MVS-compatible. (IBM.)

NetWare Communications Services Manager configures, monitors, and maintains Network communication services anywhere on the network. Provides real-time alert reception, session control, and fault and performance measurement. The package is Windows 3.x-compatible. (Novell, Inc.)

OpenNet OSI Network Management includes facilities for performance, fault reporting, and security management. The package is AT&T UNIX System V-compatible. (Pyramid Technology Corp.)

Open Management System (OMS) includes configuration and performance management utilities. The package is Sun SPARCstation/SunOS-compatible. (VitaLink Communications Corp.)

OS/Eye*Node provides for configuration management, troubleshooting, and performance analysis. The package runs on IBM RS/6000/AIX, DG AViiON/DG/UX, HP/HP-UX, SCO UNIX, Sun/SunOS, AT&T UNIX System V, and DEC/OSF/1. (Digital Analysis Corp.)

Polycenter Performance Solution centralizes monitoring of UNIX system performance information. The package runs on DEC DECsystem, DECstation, VAX/ULTRIX, OpenVMS, and Sun/SunOS. (Digital Equipment Corp.)

Probe/Net is a network performance monitor. The package runs on Sun SPARCstation/SunOS, HP/HP-UX, IBM/AIX, and SCO UNIX. (Landmark Systems Corp.)

Systems Monitor/6000 provides for fault and performance management. The package is IBM RS/6000/AIX-compatible. (IBM.)

TalkManage provides configuration, performance, and fault management. The package is Apple Macintosh-compatible. (The Distributed Technologies Corp.)

Vital Signs for LANS monitors performance for both Ethernet and token ring LANs. The package is PC-MS/DOS-compatible. (Blueline Software.)

XNETMON provides configuration management and performance management facilities. The package runs on AT&T UNIX System V; Sun/SunOS; DG/DG/&X; SCO UNIX; DEC VAX/VMS, ULTRIX; and 386/ix. (SNMP Research, Inc.)

XNETPERFMON provides performance management and security monitoring facilities. The package runs on AT&T UNIX System V; Sun/SunOS; DG/DG/&X; SCO UNIX; DEC VAX/VMS, ULTRIX; and 386/ix. (SNMP Research, Inc.)

Security Management Products

The following commercially available products can be acquired to assist the network administrator in managing security, backup and recovery, and user access to network resources:

Aria*BackupPlus provides automatic, unattended backup for UNIX and PC-based networks. It supports user-directed backup, archive, and file restoration without assistance from system administration personnel. The package is CDC-compatible. (Control Data Systems, Inc.)

Backup Architect is a backup system for Apollo Domain networks. The package runs on HP Apollo Domain/Domain/OS and HP-UX. (Workstation Solutions.)

Blockade is a network access security program that allows networks to be opened up safely to dial-in, gateways, terminals, or other remote user access. The package is IBM/MVS-, MVS/XA-, and MVS/ESA-compatible. (UTI-MACO Safeguard Systems, Inc.)

CA-ONGUARD is an access control security system. The package runs on Tandem NonStop II, TXP, EXT, VLX, CLX, and Cyclone. (Computer Associates International, Inc.)

Filesafe plus Librarian/NLM enables network administrators to back up their network. The package is PC-MS/DOS-compatible. (Mountain Network Solutions, Inc.)

GateKeeper is a network security system that provides boot protection through controlled access to hard disk. The package is PC-MS/DOS-compatible. (Rybs Electronics, Inc.)

GURUtape is a system administration program that includes backup, tape management, and restore functions. The package is Sun/SunOS-compatible. (Alida, Inc.)

LANgard Plus provides security, centralized administration, and audit trails. The package is PC-MS/DOS-compatible. (Command Software Systems, Inc.)

LANSight Support provides real-time configuration information from remote location, diagnostic and monitoring capabilities, and security support. The package is PC-MS/DOS-compatible. (Intel Corp.)

LANSweep performs unattended backup of multiple NetWare file servers. The package is PC-MS/DOS-compatible. (WBS and Associates, Inc.)

Montage provides for device configuration management and access security. The package is Windows 3.x-compatible. (Octocom Systems, Inc.)

LANtrail is an audit trail utility. The package is PC-Ms/DOS- and Sun-3 4/SunOS-compatible. (Hughes LAN Systems, Inc.)

LANVision performs security functions in an ethernet, token ring, and FDDI LANs. The package is PC-MS/DOS-compatible. (Optical Data Systems, Inc.)

NAMS provides automatic fault detection and alarming, password access, log printer and audit trail, network inventory data files, and a trouble-ticketing system. The package is DEC VAX/VMS-compatible. (CXR Dialog, Inc.)

Net/Assure is a network security system for the prevention of unauthorized use of or access to data or network. The package is PC-MS/DOS-compatible. (Cordant.)

NetSECURE is a performance diagnostic tool that simulates backup and measures feed rate or performance of data. The package is PC-MS/DOS-compatible. (Tallgrass Technologies Corp.)

Netsight Professional Enhancement monitors performance, errors, and security. The package is PC-MS/DOS-compatible. (Intel Corp.)

Network Archivist backs up and restores all Novell extended attributes. The package is PC-MS/DOS-compatible. (Palindrome Corp.)

NightShift is a network backup program that includes automatic shutdown, backup of client floppies, client cancel backup, client-excludable files, daily log file, file compression, restoration to AppleShare volume, and scheduled backups. The package is Apple Macintosh-compatible. (Transitional Technology, Inc.)

Nsure is a network backup-archive program. The package is PC-MS/DOS-compatible. (FortuNet, Inc.)

OpenNet OSI Network Management includes facilities for performance, fault reporting, and security management. The package is AT&T UNIX System V-compatible. (Pyramid Technology Corp.)

OSI 830 Global Network Management System is a network security and configuration support system The package is PC-MS/DOS-compatible. (Octocom Systems, Inc.)

QTShare performs remote network backups from a central workstation. It includes a built-in client/server password system. The package is Apple Macintosh-compatible. (Tecmar, Inc.)

Sytos Preserver for Windows provides backup, restore, and archival capabilities for individual files, directories, and entire server volumes from multiple servers and workstations. The package is Windows 3.x-compatible. (Syntron.)

TermServ is a modem security and management system that includes software dial-back capabilities, dial-in and call-back passwords, and records of all modem input/output (I/O) to file. The package is Sun/SunOS-, Pyramid-, and SCO UNIX-compatible. (Qualtrak Corp.)

UniQube 1000, UniQube 1000 Command, UniQube 400 restarts network devices that have failed and can power on/off network workstations and file servers. The package is PC-MS/DOS-compatible. (UniQube Corp.)

Uni-VIEW NMS is a graphics-based configuration management, fault isolation, and security management program. It includes security sign-on, icon-based configuration, multiwindow view, and real-time alarm processing. The package is PC-MS/DOS- and OS/2-compatible. (DSC Communications Corp.)

Workstation Option backs up, archives, and manages local DOS workstations via Novell's IPX protocol. The package is PC-MS/DOS-compatible. (Palindrome Corp.)

XNETPERFMON provides performance management and security monitoring facilities. The package runs in AT&T UNIX System V; Sun/SunOS; DG/DG/&X; SCO UNIX; DEC VAX/VMS, ULTRIX; and 386/ix. (SNMP Research, Inc.)

Glossary

abstraction   The process of isolating common characteristics of a group of classes and putting them into a higher-level class so that sharing can occur.

accounting management   A network management function defined by the International Standards Organization (ISO) that involves gathering information about the usage of various portions of the network to allocate cost to the users.

actor   Any object external to the system that is linked to the input and output data flow (e.g., a user, another system, a client, or a server).

agent   The part of a system's software that performs information retrieval and exchange on behalf of a client or server application.

algorithm   A statement of actions required to solve a problem in a finite number of steps.

application   A computer program developed for a specific data-processing system (e.g., a manufacturing information system, a financial information system, a marketing information system).

application layer   The generic term for all software which performs a user-visible function (e.g., file transfer).

asynchronous communications   A form of data transmission in which there can be variable time intervals between characters, but the bits within a character are sent with fixed time intervals.

attribute   A property or characteristic of a class that is shared by each object of the class.

backbone   The primary connective cable of a hierarchical distributed system that links individual network segments.

bandwidth   A range of frequencies recommended for transmission of data via a transmission media (cable).

baseband   A transmission technique that allows only one signal at a time to travel on a cable.

block   A sequence of continuous data transmitted as a unit.

bottom up   A technique of design and/or programming by which the lowest levels of instructions are combined to form a higher-level operation.

bridge   A local area network (LAN) interconnection device used to link two or more local or remote LANs.

broadcast   A packet delivery system that allows all hosts attached to the network to receive a copy of the sent packet.

bus   A LAN topology in which all nodes on the network share a single length of cable (backbone) running between two points.

carrier   A communication medium used to transmit information in the form of signals.

carrier sense multiple access with collision detection (CSMA/CD)   The algorithm used in ethernet networks to share the use of the LAN media.

classes   A group of objects with similar properties and behavioral characteristics and common relationships.

client   The computer which runs the programs that enables users to formulate requests for service and passes the requests to the server.

coaxial cable   A transmission medium with an outer shield that protects the cable from electromagnetic and radio-frequency interferences.

configuration management   A network management function defined by ISO that involves installing, reinitializing, and modifying hardware and software.

connections   A term used in the network environment to describe the path between two devices. (Also referred to as *network connectivity*.)

core gateways   Routers which form the principal switching nodes in Internet, a number of regional networks, and LANs.

datagram   The name for the block of information that carries in its header the network-level destination address, source address, and other protocol-specific information (e.g., routing control fields).

data-link layer   The Open Systems Interconnection (OSI) model layer that provides packet delivery functions for LANs and other wide area network (WAN) links.

DB2   A relational database management system (RDBMS) for IBM Multiple Virtual Storage (MVS) environments.

declaration   An expression in a programming language that affects the interpretation of other expressions in that language.

distributed data processing   A collection of processes that are interconnected to decentralize resources and provide an environment for the execution of application programs.

distributed database   A database that is located on a number of different computers which are often in different locations.

domain   (1) In object-oriented programming, any legal range of values that can be assigned to an object's attributes; (2) in object-oriented analysis, the set of objects which define the application; (3) in a network environment, those resources which are controlled by one or more servers.

encapsulation   (1) In object-oriented computing, the process of separating those external aspects of an object which are accessible to other objects from the internal aspects of an object that are hidden from other objects; (2) in networking, a basic protocol layering technique whereby information from a higher-level protocol is carried as the data portion of a lower-level protocol.

e-mail   A computer application which allows computer users to exchange messages and documents via electronic-mail applications on their computers.

Ethernet   A local area network standard originally developed by Xerox capable of linking ≤1024 nodes in a bus network using baseband mode of transmission at 10 megabits per second (Mbits/s), coaxial cable, bus topology, and a CSMA/CD protocol.

fault management   One of the five basic network management functions defined by ISO. It involves the detection, isolation, and correction of faults on the network system.

fiber-optic cable   A transmission medium made of glass or plastic fibers that has a high bandwidth and low susceptibility to interference.

file server   A computer which provides file storage for workstations on the network.

File Transfer Protocol (FTP)   The application-level protocol used to transfer files between two hosts on a Transmission Control Protocol/Internet Protocol (TCP/IP)-based network system.

filtering   The decision a bridge makes on every received packet to determine whether it should be continued, dropped, or forwarded.

forwarding   The process of transmitting packets received by a bridge over one or more of its other data-link ports.

frame   A block of data consisting of its own set of control information.

gateway   A high-level protocol conversion device used to enable networks using a particular protocol suite to communicate with networks running a different protocol.

high-level data-link control (HDLC)   A link protocol sometimes used to define packet boundaries and add checksum after each packet.

host   A multiuser computer that establishes an addressable node on a LAN.

hub   A central switch in a twisted-pair network in which all the nodes in the network are connected via point-to-point lines to the hub.

inheritance   The ability of an object-oriented system to transfer the attributes of a set of higher-level objects to successive lower levels within the structure or hierarchy of classes.

instances   Every object that is a member of a certain class. The current state of an instance is defined by the operations performed on the instance.

interface   The boundary between two components of a network. *Hardware interfaces* define physical connectors, signal definitions, media, and related issues. *Software interfaces* define the exact services and means of invoking those services.

internet   A collection of networks interconnected by linking devices such as routers, gateways, and bridges to operate as a single large network.

internet protocol   The network layer protocol for the TCP/IP internetwork protocol suite that provides the addressing fragmentation functions needed to allow routers to forward packets across a multiple-LAN network.

internetworking   The process of connecting together separate heterogeneous computer networks.

LAN media   Coaxial cable of various forms, shielded twisted-pair cable (TPC), unshielded twisted-pair cable (UTC), fiber optics, and even radio signals used as LAN media. See **local area network (LAN).**

layer   A conceptual level of network processing functions defined by OSI.

local area network (LAN)   A high bandwidth network designed for computer communications with a building or campus.

logical link control (LLC)   The upper sublayer of the data-link layer defined by IEEE 802 that allows higher-layer protocols to operate independently of the LAN being used.

management information base (MIB)   A specification describing all the management objects which can be accessed by a network management protocol.

media   Coaxial cable of various forms, shielded TPC, UTC, fiber optics, and even radio signals used as LAN media.

media access control (MAC)   The lower portion of the data-link layer on a LAN defined by IEEE 802.

message   A general term used to describe one of the transition stages of data as it travels over the different TCP/IP layers.

methods   Procedures that are used to create, destroy, or alter objects within an application.

middleware   The layer of software that shields applications developers from different communications protocols.

multiple access   A means of controlling transmissions over a wire or other media that allows more than one sender to transmit over that media at different times, thus sharing its use.

multiport bridges   Bridges with three or more data-link interfaces or ports that can be used to connect more than two networks together at a single point.

multiprotocol   A network node which can support more than one protocol simultaneously.

multistation   A network that allows more than one station, or network node, to be attached to the same link.

network   Communications paths and the computers, terminals, and other devices that are interconnected.

network connectivity   See **connections.**

network layer   The OSI model layer responsible for routing datagrams hop by hop through a potentially complex network of individual links or LANs.

network management systems (NMSs)   A combination of software and hardware devices that together enable management of the network.

network operating system (NOS)   The generic term for the software which is added to the workstations and file server computers to allow them to use the network.

node   A computer or other device connected to the network which can be directly addressed by other nodes.

object   (1) In C++, an entity in computer memory that contains a set of related data and performs assigned tasks by communicating with other objects; (2) in object-oriented analysis and design, an abstraction of a real-world entity defined by its procedures or informational characteristics.

object-oriented programming   A programming technique that incorporates encapsulation, polymorphism, and inheritance.

object-based programming   A programming technique that incorporates the encapsulation of data and program code, but does not support polymorphism or inheritance.

object-oriented program   The program code that supports objects, methods resolution, and inheritance.

Open System Interconnection (OSI)   The "model" or architecture proposed by ISO for use in designing computer networking protocols and systems.

operating system   A program that controls (1) the implementation of programs written by the user and (2) the operations of the peripherals associated with the program.

packet   The name of the unit of information sent by a data-link layer.

packet switching   A communication technique in which data is packetized and transmitted at variable intervals with other data.

parallel processing   The simultaneous processing of several applications or parts of applications on separate processors.

physical layer   The OSI model layer that specifies the details of the LAN or link media (e.g., transmission rate, media, signal levels, connectors).

point-to-point protocol (PPP)   A defined standard format for use of a serial telecommunications link by routers and other nodes.

polymorphism   A term used to describe how related instances can communicate to an instance of an unknown class using a single message.

presentation layer   The OSI model layer that deals with conversion of data formats from one computer to another [e.g., American Standard Code for Information Interchange (ASCII) character codes to Extended Binary Coded Decimal Interchange Code (EBCDIC)].

protocol   A collection of rules, procedures, and detailed data formats specifying how computers communicate on a network.

relational database   A database in which the individual files hold data in the form of flat files or tables.

remote   A term used to describe network devices that are managed or controlled from a network system other than the system to which they are directly connected.

repeaters   Hardware devices that regenerate LAN signals to extend the length of the network.

resource sharing   A generic term for the shared use of resources on a system or network by users or peripherals.

ring   A network topology in which all nodes are connected in a closed loop or a ring.

router   Network interconnection device that forwards packets using network-level (OSI network layer 3) addresses.

serial transmission   A method of information transfer in which each bit of a character is sent in sequence.

server   A computer that manages the data resources and performs the database engine functions such as storing, manipulating, and protecting data.

session layer   The OSI model layer that includes those functions involved in establishing communications between two applications.

Simple Network Management Protocol (SNMP)   A protocol defined to aid in managing a network that provides a means for applications on a network to obtain information from other nodes on the network.

SQL   A quasi-language and de facto standard for IBM and American National Standards Institution (ANSI) for addressing, creating, updating, or querying relational databases.

star   A LAN using a star or daisy-chain topology.

token passing   A LAN protocol which employs tokens as part of the access control mechanism.

token ring   A loop topology in which the LAN media is connected in point-to-point links from one station to the next until all stations are connected.

top-down   A method of systems design that begins with a simple overall structure and then proceeds to refine the modules and subsystems until a detailed design is produced.

Transmission Control Protocol (TCP) The primary protocol used in the Internet Protocol suite for reliable transmission of data from one host to another.

transport layer The OSI model layer responsible for the reliable delivery of the user's messages from one computer to another, including the conversion of arbitrary-length messages to the datagrams which the network layer processes.

twisted-pair wire Two individual wires wrapped around each other, forming a single cable.

use case A sequence of related transactions to be performed in a dialog between the actor and the system.

wide area network (WAN) A network that usually requires the use of telecommunications facilities provided by common carriers.

Index

ABOUT THE AUTHOR

Steve Ayer is a documentation and systems development consultant, and works for such major corporations as National Semiconductor, Fairchild Microprocessor, Fujitsu America, Westinghouse Marine Division, and Coors Brewing Company. He began his career as a satellite engineer with Lockheed Missiles & Space, and later worked as a systems development and project management seminar leader with Technical Communications Associates.

Mr. Ayer is the author or coauthor of numerous books, including the award-winning *Documenting the Software Development Process*, available from McGraw-Hill.